Clara's Kitchen

Wisdom, Memories, and Recipes
from the Great Depression

Clara's Kitchen

Clara Cannucciari

with Christopher Cannucciari

St. Martin's Press ❦ New York

www.stmartins.com

Book design by Ralph Fowler / rlf design

Photographs by Abby Lope

Library of Congress Cataloging-in-Publication Data Available Upon Request

ISBN 978-0-312-60827-9

First Edition: November 2009

10   9   8   7   6   5   4   3   2   1

This book is dedicated to Dino and Carl,

the two loves of my life.

—Clara

Contents

Acknowledgments

Clara and Christopher would like to thank the whole Cannucciari family: Nancy, Therese, John-Paul, Mark, Patrick, Henry, Carl, and Kyoko. A special thanks to Abby Cope for capturing the meals with loving care. Clara would also like to thank her brother, Sam, and everyone back at Melrose Park who remembers the old neighborhood, plus a big thanks to all of our friends in Skaneateles, New York.

This book would not have been possible without the hard work and magic of Francine LaSala, and the guidance of Sharon Bowers. We are especially grateful to Michael Flamini and everyone at St. Martin's Press for their strong vision and love of all things Clara.

Most of all we would like to thank everyone who has taken the time to watch Clara's videos. Without your support Clara's recipes might have disappeared and her stories faded away. Thank you for seeing the importance of keeping these simple meals and wisdom alive. We hope that you will pass these recipes on through the generations of your own families.

Preface

Cooking with Clara

An afternoon with our grandparents was always a magical experience, as warm golden light streamed through their kitchen windows and the aroma of something sweet wafted from the oven. They would tell timeworn stories of people and places long forgotten. They'd teach us their favorite card games and tell us how much better behaved we were than our father or mother. Their wisdom was ours for the taking, but sadly, we may have been too young to appreciate the fullness of this gift.

I had lost all but one of my grandparents before I grasped the meaning of their often repeated tales and instruction. I remember the day that I sat in the kitchen with my Nana, Clara, as she retold one of her favorite stories while I relished a magnificent plate of pasta. The recipe was as old as the story, and it dawned on me that my Nana was the last open window to my family's past. Without her we would have only a few written stories and recipes to show our children and our children's children. I immediately set to work to capture the tales she so freely spins.

Clara has so many stories that she loves to retell, but as it is for most of us, it's her childhood she loves to recollect. Clara's childhood had very little resemblance to my own. She has seen more trials and tribulations than I can imagine. Listening to her share these stories, I hear not only the hardships, but also a message of hope that has given me the confidence to share her with the rest of the world. She is indeed an optimist, raised in a time of great pessimism. I think this message touches many people in these tough times. It is a nice reaffirmation for us to hear that frugality and family are truly the keys to a good life.

The pages before you are more than a cookbook. Here is a book of experience and wisdom from a genuine survivor of America's most challenging era: the Great Depression. Clara's tales, from a time ravaged by poverty and sadness, reveal special recipes and stories to help fill the stomach and soul, and bring us back to a strong sense of family, heritage, and legacy.

I hope you will enjoy Clara's wit and wisdom as much as I do.

—CHRISTOPHER CANNUCCIARI

Clara's Kitchen

Introduction

MY NAME IS actually "Calogera" Bonfani Cannucciari, and I was born August 18, 1915. When people find out how old I am and that I lived through the Great Depression, they ask a lot of questions, especially these days. How did you live on so little—and how did you stretch out what you had? How did you eat? I tell them that it wasn't easy, but we managed. We just relied on what we *did* have—the ability to sacrifice and put our needs in perspective. To be resourceful about what we got. And by preparing and eating simple, filling foods.

These are the basic truths I've always lived by, even now into my mid-nineties. I've experienced two world wars and many other wars. I was a teenager during the Great Depression, and I survived all the recessions that followed. I have seen the world and people's attitudes change. And I've lived to become something I would never have imagined: a celebrity chef.

I'm not a trained chef. I learned to cook from my mother, who learned to cook from hers, back when she was a girl in the Old Country. My family is originally from Sicily (I am first in my family to have been born in America), and my parents brought up my younger brother, Sam, and me Sicilian, just as they had been brought up. This means they worked hard and they expected the same from us. Even in the toughest years, we got by.

When I was growing up, we lived in an Italian section of Melrose Park, a suburb of Chicago. It was so Italian, in fact, that whenever we rode the street car and the conductor came close to our stop, he'd say, "Next stop, Spaghetti Town!" We had family there, both on my mother's and father's side, but everyone in the neighborhood was like a big extended family. We knew everyone, and all of us Italians pretty much stuck together.

My father, Joseph Giuseppe Bonfani, was a carpenter and brick layer. He worked with Irish, Polish, and German Americans and learned to speak their languages. He was used to learning languages. He was born in Sicily in 1883, but when he was six, his family moved to Tunis, Africa, a French colony, where he learned to speak and read French and Arabic.

When he was twenty-three, his father died, and his mother, sisters, and their husbands all headed to America. He and his mother settled in Pennsylvania, where he became a coal miner, while his sisters and their families traveled on to Chicago. But several years later, after a mining accident that nearly left him blind, he and his mother moved

to Chicago to join the rest of their family in Melrose Park. And that's where he met my mother in 1914.

My father learned English quickly. He liked learning. He always had a book in his hand. When he was working, he was working, but when he was home he was reading. He always told us that we should learn as much as possible.

My mother was more practical-minded. She never had any education and she never cared. Born Giuseppina Di Maria in 1890 in Gratteri (a province of Palermo) she never spoke any language but Italian. Not even English.

In 1904, her sister, Lucia, got married, and a couple of years after that, Lucia, whom we always called Aunt Lucy, moved to the United States with her husband. Lucia sent for my mother in 1913, who told her own mother that she would live in the States a few years to make some money and that she'd return. She never went back. She was living with her sister and brother-in-law in Melrose Park when she met my father, and she married him the following year. I was born a year later, and my brother, Sam, a couple of years after that.

My mother was only twenty-three when she came to this country, but she was already set in her ways. Because she never wanted to learn English, we spoke only Italian at home, so I didn't speak English until I got to school. I was a little scared my first day of first grade at Our Lady

of Mount Carmel, but luckily, my cousin Mary was also in my class and she spoke both languages. It did get a little tricky, though, because we didn't sit next to each other. By the time I got to third grade, I pretty much knew English. It was simple: If I wanted to play with the other kids, I had to learn. And I really loved to play.

We usually didn't get to do our homework until after dinner. The lamp didn't move, so we had to do work wherever the light was, and that meant we'd always be together as a family each night, which was nice. We also only had one inkwell for our pens. Of course we had to go real easy on that as well. We all gathered around the downstairs light (we only had one upstairs and one down) around the table in the main room, where Sam and I did our homework and my father read; my mother would be sitting just out of the light in a chair listening to us chat away. She would answer us if we asked her something, but I think she was pretending to be awake after a day of hard work.

In addition to never learning English, my mother only cooked the meals she made in the Old Country. She just adjusted her recipes to use the ingredients that were available to us, and that were also affordable. We had potatoes with pasta and hot dogs with Italian bread. A mix of both worlds. Everything was so delicious. I didn't appreciate it back then, but I miss the way she used to cook now. I learned to cook by watching her and my aunts.

In the 1920s, my father was working nights in a steel factory in Melrose Park, Illinois. It wasn't a great job, not like when he was in construction. He worked all the time and for a miserable wage. We never saw him, and for a check we couldn't even pay for anything with. He was laid off from there in 1929, just at the start of the Great Depression.

It was such a terrible time. No one had work—no one was hiring. My father didn't work again for another six years. But he was resourceful. While he was out of work, he arranged to pick vegetables, getting paid one bushel of vegetables a day instead of money. My mother would promptly jar and can most of these just in case the following month Dad wouldn't get even the vegetables. We all had to pull together. We all struggled. We all sacrificed. We just tightened our belts and learned to make do on what was available to us.

Shanty towns shot up everywhere, where people actually lived in shacks, people who used to live in the houses in our neighborhood. Lots of people lost their homes back then, but we were lucky. We had no mortgage and we also had a small apartment we could rent out to make extra money. But there were still the taxes to pay, and lots of people, including my mother's sister, my aunt Lucy, and her family, ended up losing their homes because of that. If we couldn't pay the taxes, we'd lose our home, too.

By 1931, we were suffering so much that my parents couldn't even afford the clothes I needed to wear to attend school. My mother suffered badly from rheumatoid arthritis and wasn't able to work because of it. My brother was too young to leave school to get a job, but, luckily, I was not. I

was old enough by then that I could leave school and help bring money into the house. I left Proviso East High School in the middle of my sophomore year to get a job.

I worked first as a maid, earning $25 a month, but left that after six months. Next I sewed blouses from home, earning $2 for every two dozen blouses completed. After that, I worked at the Jefferson Electric factory making radio coils, but was fired by a boss who didn't like me, and was out of work for a long time. It wasn't because I wasn't looking. I was always looking. But there were no jobs. One day I stopped at every factory between Melrose Park and Chicago (a fifteen-mile stretch) without a single offer. I eventually found work at the Hostess Twinkie factory in Oak Park.

It wasn't easy back then. But the lessons I learned, when money was tight and hard work and creativity was all we had, I have carried with me my entire life. I applied them to my work and to raising my own family. I believe those days made me who I am today, and that part of the reason I have made it this far is that surviving those hardships made me strong enough to survive anything.

———————

When my grandson Christopher told me he wanted to film me making my recipes, I thought, "Who wants to see that?" But after all the positive feedback I've been getting, I understand. Times are tough now, like they were back when I was growing up. People need tips and encouragement to survive these thin times, and I'm happy to have a way to help.

In this book, I'll share my memories with you of growing up and getting by during the Great Depression and the years that followed, and how the lessons I learned have stayed with me to this very day. I'll share recipes for the meals I learned to cook in my mother's kitchen, and how to fill your family up spending as little as fifty cents a meal. I'll also add years to your life, sharing advice for saving money and staying healthy and strong into your nineties. And if you make the meal different, it's not bad, it'll be your style.

My name is Clara Cannucciari and I am ninety-four years old. Welcome to my kitchen.

CHAPTER ONE

Goods from the Garden and "Found" Foods

ESPECIALLY IN THE LEAN YEARS of the Depression, we lived on vegetables and, and it kept us plenty strong and healthy for all the hard work at hand. Meat was a treat, but vegetables were our staples.

When I was a kid, my father kept a garden in the backyard, which we helped him keep up, and my mother would take the vegetables we grew and make them into all kinds of meals. Not just side dishes like you would today. The vegetables, made with pasta or on their own, were the main event. Meat was too hard to come by most of the time. We had to stretch out whatever we had for as long as we could, so whatever we couldn't eat, my mother would can and preserve for winter. Sometimes we'd eat stuff that grew wild,

like burdock and dandelions and mushrooms. We'd find it, and Ma would clean and cook it.

My father would plant vegetables all summer. Ma would take out the seeds, dry them out, and then my father would plant them again. And that's how we kept our garden growing. Whatever was left over, my mother would can. We ate really well in the Depression, and throughout the year, because of that. Here are some of my favorite recipes Ma made with the vegetables we grew.

Swiss Chard with Garlic

I T'S EASY TO FORGET about nutrition when your pockets are empty, but where there's dirt, there's food—healthy, nutritious food. Back in the Depression, lots of people grew gardens to eat from, including us. Some people would grow gardens in the summer and then go through the streets and try and sell their stuff. Buying someone else's vegetables was too expensive for us, but we still needed to eat.

A couple of times, my father stood in line for food the government supplied, but he hated it. He was very proud and self-reliant, and he would rather go without than take handouts. I think he went twice and then never again. Instead, my father took matters into his own hands and kept a great big garden in our backyard. He grew just about everything there. Carrots, escarole, spinach, asparagus, radishes, beans, eggplant, peppers, Swiss chard, you name it. We ate so healthy with all those vegetables and we weren't even trying. And we worked hard helping him keep that garden in shape. No wonder we all live so long—my brother and I are both healthy and strong and in our nineties!

Swiss chard was good, but it was always a little bitter for me, so Ma would always add some garlic to give it a little extra something. You can toss this over pasta or serve it as a side for a meat dish.

You will need

> 1 bunch Swiss chard
> 1 tablespoon olive oil
> 1 clove garlic, minced
> Salt and pepper

1. Bring a large pot of water to the boil.
2. Thoroughly rinse the Swiss chard, removing most of the tough stems (but leave some if they look like they will be tender).
3. Add the Swiss chard to the pot. Boil 5 minutes, then drain and set aside. When it's cool enough to handle, squeeze it between your hands to get all the extra water out of the chard.
4. Add the oil to a medium frying pan set over medium heat. Add the garlic and sauté until the garlic turns a very light brown.
5. Add the Swiss chard and sauté until tender—about 5 to 7 minutes. Season with salt and pepper.

Fried Potatoes and Vegetables

· Serves 4 ·

WINTERS WERE TOUGH in the Midwest, then and now. I never liked winter. And I hate snow. It's white, but it darkens your heart. Especially when you have to walk through piles of it with holes in your stockings to get to school.

But it did have one upside for us. In winter, when there was snow and ice, we'd be able to save food longer. We didn't have a refrigerator or even an icebox when I was a kid, and we'd have to eat everything or else it'd go bad. But in the wintertime, we could store our food outside, digging a hole in the snow and ice. Mom would say: "Sam, go out and get the leftover roast from last night. It's buried out by the fence." I laugh about it now, but it was kind of sad.

Later, though, we had an icebox. The iceman would come and bring us fifty pounds of ice. There was a tray underneath that Sam and I were supposed to remember to empty. We'd forget about it all the time and get such a whuppin' if all that water ended up on the floor. They sure didn't "spare the rod" in those days.

No, we didn't have most of the modern conveniences everyone has today. We relied on canning and jarring to preserve our food when we couldn't "ice" it. We didn't have a washing machine until after the Depression. We used to wash clothes with a washboard, which I still have hanging in my home. Because of my mother's arthritis, she would boil the clothes, but then it would be up to me to scrub them against the washboard and wring them out through a hand-cranked wringer. It was pretty hard to do.

We had indoor plumbing, but we didn't have central heat. We warmed our house with a wood-burning stove and furnace, but because my parents always wanted to save coal and wood, it was always cold in the house. And they didn't want to use up what they had in case it got colder. We'd sit in front of the stove and the front of us would be warm, but our backs would freeze. Then we'd turn around and warm our backs, and our fronts would freeze. Those were the good old days, before we had a real furnace.

The only lights we had were from our two kerosene lamps, but in the 1920s, we got gaslights. They put in pipes and almost every room had a light. The lights would be on the side of the wall and there would be little jets of gas that you would light by putting a match there. There would be

the little flicker of gaslight and we thought this was so bright. In the 1930s, our house got wired with electricity and we had our first lightbulbs. When we turned them on for the first time we thought, "Oh my gosh, it's like daylight!" Maybe it was 20 or 15 watts, but we thought it was so bright. (And we left in the gaslights just in case we lost the lightbulbs.)

Fried Potatoes and Vegetables is a hearty meal that's good in the winter because it's filling and warms you from the inside. Turnips are in season from November to April, so they're good to cook with in winter, but they can be stored a long time, so this meal can be eaten any time of the year.

You will need

4 tablespoons vegetable oil

2 large potatoes, peeled and cut into 1-inch cubes

1 turnip, peeled and cut into 1-inch cubes

2 carrots, peeled and cut into 1-inch cubes

½ red onion, diced

1 celery stalk (leaves and all), chopped

1 tomato, chopped

½ head escarole, chopped

Salt and pepper

Pecorino Romano cheese

1. Pour the vegetable oil into a frying pan and set it over medium heat Add the potatoes, turnip, carrots, and onion and sauté slowly, about 15 minutes, but don't mix the vegetables too much or they won't brown.

2. Add the chopped celery and sauté for another 15 minutes, or until the potatoes are brown on all sides.

3. Add the tomato and escarole and continue to cook for 5 minutes. Turn off heat.

4. Season with salt and pepper to taste, and sprinkle with cheese. Serve immediately.

Squash with Eggs

W E MADE A LOT OF MEALS with eggs because they weren't just cheap, they were practically free. Back in those days, we all had our own chickens, which we kept in the yard. It was pretty normal to have a few chickens running around the yard back then, but they probably wouldn't allow that anymore. So we always had our own eggs. And then sometimes for Sunday dinner, we'd kill a chicken. But that was rare. We needed the eggs!

Squash was one of the vegetables we grew in our garden, and there was always plenty of it to go around. So free eggs and free vegetables made Squash and Eggs one of our most delicious meals. Maybe more delicious because it didn't cost anything but the time it took to fry it up.

You will need

> 4 tablespoons vegetable oil
> 3 large yellow summer squash, diced
> 12 large eggs
> Salt and pepper
> Pecorino Romano cheese, optional

1. Heat the vegetable oil in a large frying pan over medium to high heat. Add the squash to the oil and sauté for about 10 minutes, or until tender.

2. Crack the eggs into the pan with the squash (for one-pot cooking) and scramble until they achieve the desired texture.

3. Remove the pan from the heat, and add salt and pepper to taste. I also like to top this with a little Pecorino Romano cheese.

Take It from Me

If you don't think you have time to exercise, just clean your kitchen. I think it's kind of silly—the people jogging. Scrubbing my floors and counters makes everything strong, and my kitchen looks good.

Spinach and Rice

· Serves 4 ·

WHEN I WAS A GIRL, I was a tomboy. I loved playing active games, running around and using up a lot of energy. After school, some of the girls played house or with dolls, but I liked playing tag or hide-and-seek. And pretty much every time we were playing, someone would ask: "Do you want to play baseball?" I always wanted to play baseball. But I'd get skinned if I got my school clothes dirty, so I'd say, "Yeah! I'll be out in a minute," and then I'd race home, take off my school dress, and put on a play dress.

I used to play a lot of baseball. Boys and girls would play together and we would play in the streets. Even in high school, I was still playing baseball with the boys. I didn't date any of them, but we were always hanging around together. The boys never asked what I was doing playing with them. I guess I just belonged with them. They would get into trouble, and I'd be with them, but when it got dark we'd all go home or our mothers would give us a lickin'. Sometimes I used to get one anyway. "Why don't you play dolls with the girls?" she'd ask me. But I didn't say anything. Baseball was just more fun.

It also meant needing lots of pep, so all those vegetables we were eating really helped—especially all that spinach. Here's a simple meal that can help to build up your strength, load you up with vitamins, and even though it's low in fat, will make you feel full.

You will need

6 cups raw spinach
1 cup rice
2 tablespoons olive oil
Salt and pepper

1. Cook the rice according to the manufacturer's directions—usually 2 cups of water for 1 cup of rice. Cover and simmer for about 20 minutes.

2. In a separate pot, boil 3 cups of water and add the spinach. Cook for 3 minutes and drain.

3. When the rice is cooked, combine it with the spinach. Add the oil and salt and pepper to taste. Stir and serve.

Spinach Omelet

· Serves 4 ·

THE PROBLEM with playing baseball after school was that you really couldn't play in a dress, and girls didn't wear pants back then. But I had a trick so I wouldn't keep tripping over my dress. I'd tuck my dress into my bloomers, which kind of made them look like pants. If you don't know, bloomers were long underwear with an elastic waist. So I guess you could say I was just running around in my underwear, which my mother didn't like very much at all. Whenever she caught me like that, she'd give me a good lickin' on the rear. But it was worth it. It really made playing ball a lot easier.

I also used to climb telephone poles a lot to get a view of the neighborhood, and I'd have to tuck my dress into my bloomers to do this, too. And when my mother would see me on the telephone pole, she'd go crazy and holler: "What's the matter with you, come in the house!" And I would get down, slowly, because I knew what was coming to me.

One time she got so mad, she came outside and stood under

the pole. But she was very calm. "Clay, why don't you come down and come inside?" she asked me.

So I said, "No, you're going to hit me."

And she said, smiling and nice. "I'm not going to hit you, just come inside." So I came down and when she got a hold of me, boy, did I ever get it. It was dangerous now that I think of it. She was probably worried like crazy. But the view from up there was worth it.

So I got a lickin', but I never got sent to bed without supper. Weeknight meals were simple, but filling, and we'd have Spinach Omelet a lot. Here's how she made it.

You will need

> 2 tablespoons vegetable oil
> 4 cups large-leaf spinach
> 8 large eggs
> Salt and pepper

1. Heat the vegetable oil in a large frying pan over medium heat.

2. Rinse the spinach and pat dry with a kitchen towel or paper towel. Add the spinach to the oil and sauté until it wilts down, about 2 minutes.

3. Break the eggs into a bowl and whisk. Add the eggs to the wilted spinach and let them fill the whole pan. Season with salt and pepper.

4. Turn down the heat and let the eggs set. When they start to get solid, carefully turn the omelet over. Heat until the eggs are fully cooked. Divide into four parts and serve.

Sam's Favorite Green Beans

• Serves 4 •

M Y BROTHER, SAM, and I had the same relationship lots of brothers and sisters have when they grow up close in age and have to share everything. Sam was just the opposite of me. I was loud and always getting into trouble, while Sam was quiet and calm.

He played a really bad trick on me once. I don't know what got into him, but one day he put a garden snake in an envelope with my name and address on it and stuffed it into our mailbox. I was so excited to get mail, I picked it up and couldn't wait to tear it open. And then I realized there was something wiggly moving inside the envelope. When I opened it, did I ever get a good scare! And he got himself a

pretty good whupping for that one. He didn't get punished or have to go to bed without dinner or anything like that. Mom took a more direct approach with her "lessons." It's funny to think about now, but if we were growing up these days and she ever hit us like that, she'd probably go to jail.

Anyway, Sam was happy to have his whupping and get it

out of the way because that night we were having his favorite green beans. He used to really love these, but I think it was because he always hoped a roast chicken would somehow appear when my mother served them. They do actually go perfect with Roast Chicken (page 137), which I think was really Sam's favorite.

You will need

½ pound green beans, cleaned and trimmed
2 teaspoons olive oil
½ teaspoon lemon juice
Salt and pepper

1. Bring a pot of water to the boil over high heat, and add the beans. Boil for about 6 minutes. Drain and give them a quick rinse in cold running water to return the snap to the beans.

2. Put the beans in a bowl, toss with the olive oil, lemon juice, and salt and pepper to taste, and serve.

Take It from Me

Lemon juice can be used to pep anything up, from a salad dressing to steak, and can also be used as a cheap, safe cleaner for your hands or your countertops. Lemon zest gives a bright lemon flavor to anything you add it to. So I always have lemons in the house.

Hand-Squeezed Lemonade

· Serves 4 ·

IF YOU HAVE LEMONS LEFT OVER, treat yourself to lemonade. Even though lemons were cheap at three for a quarter, sugar was expensive in the Depression. So the lemonade was always tart, but good on a hot day.

You will need

> 2 lemons
> 4 cups water
> Plenty of ice
> ¼ cup sugar
> 4 fresh mint leaves

Cut the lemons in half and squeeze the juice into a pitcher. Add the water and ice. Put in the sugar and mix with a wooden spoon until the sugar is dissolved. Top with the fresh mint and serve.

Traditional Eggplant Parmesan

· Serves 4 ·

I TOLD YOU MY MOTHER made a lot of traditional Italian meals, using American ingredients when she had to, improvising the same way she improvised with English. Eggplant Parmesan was one of her signature dishes, and she was very traditional about it. She never strayed from the old ways on this dish. She never strayed away from the old ways about a lot of things. For instance, she never wore a pair of pants a day in her life and was disgusted when women

started wearing them. Especially when I started wearing them.

I had never worn pants in my life before I started working in the factory, but everyone had to wear pants at the plant. Though I'd wear pants while I was at work, I was embarrassed to wear slacks on my way home. And forget about coming home wearing them. I'd try to change out of them and back into a skirt or dress before I left the factory. Sometimes I would forget to bring a dress and I would have to walk home in slacks. People wouldn't say anything to me, but the way they looked at me, I know they thought I was strange. "What is that girl wearing?"

Little by little that started to change. During the Depression so many women were working in the factories, wearing pants started to come into fashion, and pretty soon everyone was wearing pants. Except for my mother. She was of the old school, the real old school. And stubborn about it. If I ever came home from the factory with pants on, and my mom had people over, she got so embarrassed.

"Ma, everybody wears pants," I'd say to her.

And she'd say to me: "I don't care about everybody, I don't want you to be wearing them."

The same went for the Eggplant Parmesan. I loved the way she cooked it, but when I got older, I learned that a lot of people bread and flour the eggplant, and dress it up all kinds of ways. But try telling that to my mother.

I really like the traditional style—the way Ma made it. And I don't dress it up or make it fancy or anything like that. I like to just fry it and top it with some good tomato sauce.

Also I never use parmesan cheese, I use what my mother used, Pecorino Romano. But I do wear pants most of the time. And that's that.

You will need

I large Italian eggplant
½ cup vegetable oil
¾ cup tomato sauce (see the
    Di Maria Family Sauce, page 94)
8 tablespoons Pecorino Romano
    cheese

1. Slice the eggplant into rounds, about ¼ inch thick. (You should end up with about 12 slices.) If you want, salt the slices for about an hour, then rinse. This will take out the bitter water and also give the flavor a little zip.

2. Heat the vegetable oil in a large pan over medium-high heat. Place one of the end slices of the eggplant in the oil; when the oil bubbles around it, the oil is ready for frying.

3. Fry the slices in batches, 10 to 12 minutes on one side, then 6 minutes on the other. (Flip the eggplant slices carefully, as the softer they get, the easier they fall apart.)

4. Remove the eggplant slices and drain them between paper towels, removing the excess oil from both sides of the slices.

5. When drained, arrange the slices on a serving platter and top each with about 1 tablespoon of tomato sauce and 2 teaspoons Pecorino Romano cheese.

While the Water Boils . . . Bunco

Everyone went crazy over Bunco during the Depression, and I liked it, too. The game was fun, but everyone was always so serious about it in the giant halls where everyone played. No one ever talked. They'd just play. I guess it's because the games were being played for money and there was nothing fun about that kind of thing then. Anyway, when you play, talk as much as you want. Or you can play with people you don't like to talk to. You need three six-sided dice and a pen and paper. Here's how it works.

In a nutshell: Two to four players take turns rolling three dice, trying to roll the side of the dice corresponding to that round's number. For instance, in the first round, you want to roll ones on all three dice. The first to reach 21 wins the round. There are six rounds and whoever wins the most rounds is the "Big Winner."

You will need
3 dice

Round 1
The goal of the first round is to roll ones. If you get 1 one, you get 1 point and you get to roll again. If you roll 2 ones, that's 2 points and you keep rolling. If you roll no ones, you keep your

score, but you hand over the dice to the person on your left. This goes on until someone reaches 21 and wins the round.

If you roll 3 ones, that's BUNCO, so make sure you yell it out! If someone gets BUNCO then they automatically win. BUNCO only applies to the number of the given round, in this instance, ones. If you were to roll 3 fives or 3 fours, etc, you get 5 points for getting a triplet, and then you roll again. Once a player has either reached 21 or rolled a BUNCO, the first round is over.

Round 2

In the second round, everyone tries to roll twos. The same rules apply. If you roll 1 or 2 twos you get 1 or 2 points and get to keep rolling. If you roll no twos, you keep the points you already earned, but your turn's over. Now if you roll 3 ones, it is not BUNCO, it's a triplet, and you get 5 points and another turn. But if you roll 3 twos, you get BUNCO! The first person to get to 21 points or BUNCO wins this round and records a win for this round.

And so forth

Continue through the rest of the numbers of the dice all the way to round 6, and whoever wins the most rounds wins the game. To break a tie, the players who are tied play one extra round. The side of the die used for this bonus round is decided by the roll of a single die before the bonus round is played.

Delicious Dandelions

We didn't always find our food in the grocery store. My two uncles owned grocery stores, and we'd get some there. But just because they owned the stores didn't mean we'd catch a break. So we didn't always buy the food we ate. Sometimes we couldn't—there just wasn't enough money at the end of the week to afford groceries. Sometimes we'd just have to eat whatever we found growing wild. Where some people maybe saw weeds, we saw dinner. But it was good.

Around the end of April is when the dandelions started to sprout. We headed out to our yard and picked them, eating the leaves (you have to clean and soak them before eating them!). My father was pretty happy about that—it saved him some time on weeding. My mother was also happy to have something to cook. She'd make all kinds of meals from them.

Take a large bowl and paring knife outside. Look for leaves that are green and healthy, and use your knife to uproot them. Cut the weed out at the start of the root and remove the flower.

Once you have filled your bowl, head inside to clean the dandelions. With your paring knife, carefully trim off any dirt, root, flowers, or wilted leaves. Try not to cut off too much of the bottoms or your leaves will come apart. Throw away the waste and rinse out the good parts. Rinse again and let soak for about a half hour. Take the leaves out of the water carefully so that the dirt stays in the water. Discard the dirty water and rinse the bowl well. Rinse and soak three to four more times to ensure that the weeds are nice and clean.

Dandelion Salad

THIS IS A GREAT SALAD you can make right from your yard. It's delicious, and it's basically free.

You will need

5 cups dandelion leaves, cleaned
2 teaspoons olive oil
Juice of 1 lemon
Salt and pepper

Put the clean dandelions in a salad bowl and toss with olive oil, lemon juice, and salt and pepper to taste.

Cooked Dandelion Leaves

YOU CAN ALSO COOK the leaves for a satisfying side dish, a quick hot snack, or to pep up a sandwich.

You will need

> 5 cups dandelion leaves, cleaned
> 2 teaspoons olive oil
> Juice of 1 lemon
> Salt and pepper

Bring 4 cups of water to the boil and add the cleaned dandelion leaves. Cook 3 to 5 minutes, or until tender. Drain and squeeze the excess water from the leaves. Toss the leaves with olive oil, lemon juice, and salt and pepper to taste.

Found Fried Foods

Burdock was something we had a lot, because it grew all over the place—behind the shed—anywhere, really. Burdock is a weed, and weeds grow everywhere. There was always a lot of burdock around at the end of May. I remember this from my days working at the Hostess Twinkie factory.

I used to pass the fields at Melrose Park and there it all was—miles of burdock and also dandelions and even mushrooms sometimes if you looked hard enough. I'd stop at the fields on my way back after my shift, fill up a big sack, and carry whatever I could stuff into the bag back home with me. We'd eat for nights on that. And sometimes people would come around with wild mushrooms that they would pick from the woods.

We weren't the only ones in my neighborhood to eat burdock. All the Italians used to pick it and eat it. The Germans in the neighborhood never understood it. "What are ya gonna do with that?" they'd ask us.

Of course, my mother had some other ideas about the Germans. Sure, she liked how clean they were. They were so clean, they even scrubbed the sidewalks in front of their houses, and the German lady across the street was always washing her windows. But she didn't trust them. "Don't go by the Germans," she'd say. I don't think she trusted anyone who wasn't Italian.

Fried Burdock

• Serves 4 •

You will need

4 stalks burdock
½ cup vegetable oil
1 large egg
2 cups bread crumbs
½ teaspoon salt
½ teaspoon pepper
One 8-ounce can tomato sauce (or 1 cup leftover sauce
   if you've got it)

1. Soak the burdock plants in a bowl of water for about a half an hour to clean. Separate out the stalks and discard the rest. Cut the stalks into 3- to 4-inch-long pieces.

2. Boil the stalks in a large pot of salted water until tender, about 10 minutes. While the burdock boils, pour the oil into a large frying pan and set it over medium heat.

3. Crack and whisk the egg in a large bowl, and on a separate plate, combine the bread crumbs, salt, and pepper. Dip the cooked burdock in the egg, then lightly dredge it in the bread-crumb mixture, shaking off the excess crumbs.

4. When the oil is heated to the point that it's just hot enough to start smoking, drop in the breaded stalks. Fry 4 minutes per side, or until brown and crisp.

5. Drain the burdock on paper towels and serve. (Or, better yet, drain on a rag that you can wash and use again.)

Fried Mushrooms with Red Sauce

Y OU CAN SERVE these open-faced on a generous slice of bread or toss with pasta or rice.

You will need

4 cups mushrooms
3 tablespoons olive oil
2 tablespoons tomato sauce
Salt and pepper

1. Clean the mushrooms well and slice them.

2. Heat the olive oil in a large frying pan over medium-high heat. When the oil is heated to the point that it's just hot enough to start smoking, drop in the mushrooms.

3. Turn the heat down to medium and sauté about 20 minutes, stirring occasionally.

4. Turn off the heat and stir in the tomato sauce. Season with salt and pepper to taste.

Take It from Me

How do you know if the mushrooms you found are poisonous? My mother believed if you put a quarter in the pan with the mushrooms, and the coin turned black, the mushrooms were no good. While we all survived, you're probably best off "finding" your mushrooms in the grocery store.

CHAPTER TWO

Bread, the Magic Filler

I NEVER THROW ANYTHING OUT. I work in my small back-yard garden with the same tools my father used. They're still good. I guess in those days, things were made to last. No one bought new tools every year like they do today. My family buys me new tools, but I just like using the old ones. The same goes for the pots and pans I use in my kitchen. They are all my mother's. I've got one pot with a missing handle, and people are always asking, "Why don't you throw that thing away?" And I say it's in perfect condition. If I can't cook with it, I can use it as a sugar bowl. I have an attachment to things. Favorite pots and pans I use for different things. One for pasta and garlic. One for boiling vegetables.

My stove is old. My wallpaper is old. It's the same wallpaper from when I moved here and I never changed it. Why would I change it? I just keep it clean. If you take better care of things, you can hold on to them longer. That's how I still

run things. If it works, I keep it. If it doesn't, I see if I can use it for something else. If I can't, and I usually can, I toss it.

And that's kind of how I deal with food. If it's totally rotten, sure, out it goes. But if only part of it's rotten, I cut out the bad part and eat what's left. If I have leftovers—if something was a good dinner three nights ago, it's probably a great sandwich tonight. If it was a tasty side dish last week, it could be a tasty pizza topping tomorrow. That's how we did it back then. That's how I still do it today.

Ma's Sunday Bread

· **Makes 6 loaves** ·

PROBABLY THE ONLY THING we ever had that was "new" or "fresh" was the fresh bread my mother would bake for us twice a week. Otherwise, everything was salvaged—repurposed and reused. We would save everything. If something came to our house in a box, we'd save the box, the packaging, even the string that held it closed. The crates that brought our yearly grapes for wine could be reused to store other things we saved, like the jars and cans my mother used for storing food until they cracked or rusted.

And sometimes even then. As long as something could be used for some kind of purpose, we kept it.

But every week, my mother would make six loaves of bread, and every week, we went through it. Especially during the Depression. We didn't really eat breakfast back then. Not like people these days. We'd pretty much have coffee with evaporated milk and a slice of Ma's bread. But even today, that's what I like to have. But making bread from scratch is surely a lot of work. No wonder my mom used to be crabby a lot.

We had a stove in the basement and sometimes she'd make the bread there. It wasn't easy for her, though, because of her arthritis. Sometimes she'd look at me and say "Clay," because that's what she called me, "you make the bread today." And I did. And it wasn't bad. I'm glad I was able to make it then because now I know how to make it today.

Bread may not be simple to make but it's cheap, and it's filling, and we made sandwiches all the time—the trick being to find something to put between the slices of bread.

You will need

> 9 cups all-purpose flour, plus flour for dusting
> 6 teaspoons rapid-rise yeast
> 3½ cups warm water, approximately
> 8 tablespoons olive oil
> 1½ tablespoons salt

1. Pour the flour into a large bowl and dig out a well in the middle of the pile.

2. Add the yeast, 1 cup of water, and olive oil to the well. Break up the yeast with your hands and let it melt into the mixture. After the yeast becomes incorporated with the flour, slowly mix everything together. Gradually add in 1½ tablespoons of salt.

3. With your hands, knead the ingredients together, adding more water as you go to make the mass more doughy. In all, you'll be adding about 3½ cups of warm water. This

Take It from Me

Sometimes people like to add a little moisture to the oven
when you bake bread. You don't have to, but if you decide
you want to try it, there are two techniques you can try:
First, you can set an oven-safe plate in the bottom of the
oven with some water in it. Or, you can use a spray bottle,
spritzing 5 minutes after you put the bread in the oven,
and then again 10 minutes later. Ma never did it this way,
but some people swear by it. Really, it's up to you.

should take about 20 minutes of continuous kneading. (Pretend you're mad at someone. This will help the time go faster.)

4. When it becomes springy in texture, cover the bowl with a damp dish towel and let rise 1 to 1½ hours. *Do not refrigerate.*

5. After the dough rises, punch it down and divide equally among 6 loaf pans, flattening each out into individual loaves to fit the pans.

6. Cover each of the 6 pans with a warm dish towel and set aside again on the counter. *Do not refrigerate.* Let rise an additional 15 to 30 minutes in the covered pans.

7. Preheat the oven to 450°F.

8. Once the loaves have fully risen the second time, cut small slits in the tops of each of them and bake at 450°F for 40 to 45 minutes. Their crusts will be golden when they are done.

9. Carefully remove the loaves from the oven and cool, first in their pans for about 30 minutes, and then on a rack for an additional 30 to 40 minutes.

Garlic Bread

H ERE'S A WAY TO USE one of the loaves for a special meal.

You will need

1 loaf fresh bread

5 cloves garlic, minced

2 tablespoons butter, at room temperature

1. Preheat the oven to broil. Cut the loaf in half lengthwise.

2. With the back of a spoon, spread the garlic over the cut sides of the bread and mince the butter onto the bread.

3. Place the bread under the broiler for 5 to 8 minutes, keeping a close eye on it to make sure it doesn't burn. It's done when it turns a nice golden color. Cut into slices and serve.

Leftover Dough Pizza

SOMETIMES MY MOTHER would cut off a piece of dough when she made her bread and save it to make pizza. Sometimes it would be waiting for us when we got home from school. It was a really special treat.

You will need

> 14 ounces fresh bread dough
> Flour
> 1 teaspoon olive oil
> ½ cup leftover tomato sauce
>   (see the Di Maria Family Sauce, page 94)
> 3 anchovies (or other topping of your choice)
> Pecorino Romano cheese
> 1½ ounces fresh mozzarella, sliced
> 4 fresh basil leaves

1. Preheat the oven to 350°F. Roll out the dough on a broad wooden surface lightly dusted with flour. Keep rolling evenly on all sides and flip the dough over, adding a fresh dusting of flour. Roll the dough out into a 12-inch circle.

2. Spread the oil evenly on a round pizza pan, and carefully place the dough round on the pan. Pat the dough down with your fingers to stretch it to the edges of the pan and even it out.

3. With the back of a spoon, evenly spread the tomato sauce over the dough, leaving about a ½-inch border at the edge.

4. Break up the anchovies (or topping of your choice) into small bits and distribute them evenly over the pizza. Top the pizza with an even sprinkling of Pecorino Romano cheese. Place the sliced mozzarella on top of the grated cheese.

5. Bake the pizza in the preheated oven for about 15 minutes, then place the fresh basil leaves on top, either tearing them into small pieces with your fingers or using the full leaves. Return the pizza to the oven and bake an additional 5 to 7 minutes, or until the edge is a light brown color.

6. Let the pizza rest 5 minutes before slicing and serving.

Fried Dough

ONE OF THE THINGS we used to really enjoy in the warmer weather was the summer street festival. There was one year, though, where there was a shoot-out with some gangsters in the neighborhood and the cops came and cleared everyone out. That year wasn't that much fun. But most years were. And especially for the food. We'd have all kinds of treats there, including Italian Ice (see page 158). And sometimes we'd bring our own treat to sell, like Fried Dough.

Basically, all it was really was pizza dough that was stretched out, dropped into very hot oil, and fried until it was crisp on the outside, but soft and warm on the inside. We'd sprinkle it with powdered sugar or salt, and it was delicious. I liked the salted dough the best. Other people have tried it with some tomato sauce spooned on and you might like it that way. See what works for you.

You will need

Vegetable oil for frying
Bread dough (see page 45)
Flour
Sugar, salt, or tomato sauce for topping

1. Pour the oil into a small saucepan so the oil comes about 1½ to 2 inches up the sides. Place it on the stove over medium heat, and let the oil heat slowly and evenly.

2. Place the dough on a plate and sprinkle it lightly with flour (to prevent it from sticking). Cut the dough into 6 equal pieces.

3. Roll the dough into small balls or cubes as pictured on page 53.

4. When the oil is hot, carefully place the dough, one piece at a time, into the oil, and deep-fry for about 30 seconds to 1 minute on each side, until light brown and crisp. Remove with tongs and place on a plate.

5. Repeat these steps with the remaining pieces of dough.

6. Add your choice of toppings and serve.

Potatoes and Eggs Sandwich

DURING THE DEPRESSION, we didn't have much, but one of the other things we had plenty of were potatoes. We used to buy them by the 100-pound sack. My father would buy a sack of everything—a sack of potatoes, a sack of flour—and I remember that potatoes were a dollar

a sack. A dollar was a lot of money back then, but it was money well spent. Just about everything we ate had potatoes in it. None of it ever went to waste. If we had a bad potato, we just cut the bad part out and ate the rest. They may not be glamorous, but potatoes are cheap, they can be stored for months, and they'll keep the wolf off your back when times are tough. So potatoes, combined with the other thing we always had—eggs—made for a satisfying and frequent meal in our house.

You will need

2 tablespoons vegetable oil
3 to 4 potatoes, peeled and cubed
8 large eggs
Salt and pepper
8 slices bread, thickly cut and lightly toasted

1. Heat the vegetable oil in a large pan over medium-high heat. Add the potatoes to the oil and sauté for about 20 minutes, or until soft and golden brown.

2. Crack the eggs into the pan with the potatoes and stir in the eggs until they become scrambled and golden in color. Add salt and pepper to taste.

3. Cool slightly. Spoon between slices of bread and enjoy.

Peppers and Eggs Sandwich

• Serves 2 •

I N GRAMMAR SCHOOL most kids went home for lunch. When we got to high school, Sam and I brought our lunch, like most of the other kids. I remember people used to put crazy things between bread and call it a sandwich. One of my aunts used to make lard sandwiches. And then there was this German girl who used to come to school with spaghetti sandwiches. She'd always want to trade me. Only once I fell for it before I knew what she had. She asked and she asked and I finally gave in and gave her my Peppers and Eggs Sandwich. Then I opened her lunch bag and thought, "Are you kidding me?"

My mother's Peppers and Eggs Sandwich always got a lot of attention when my brother and I took it to school. We always carried our lunch in a brown paper bag, and when we had Peppers and Eggs, the olive oil would always leak through the bag and everyone wanted to trade with me. But I was so disappointed after that spaghetti sandwich, I decided never again—I'm not trading with anybody.

You will need

> 3 large bell peppers (red, yellow, orange)
> Olive oil
> 4 large eggs
> 4 thick slices bread

1. Clean the peppers, removing the stems and seeds, and rinsing well. Slice each pepper into thick (roughly ¾ inch) strips.

2. Add the peppers and some olive oil to the pan—not too much oil, though. Just enough to coat the peppers.

3. Saute the peppers first over high heat, then lower the heat as the peppers begin to brown.

4. In a separate bowl, crack the eggs and whisk them. When the peppers are soft, about 10 minutes, fold in the eggs.

5. Turn off the heat and let cook in its own heat about 5 minutes, or until the eggs are firm.

6. Place the pepper and egg mixture between the bread slices, or serve open-faced.

Roast Asparagus Sandwich

L IKE TODAY, asparagus could be really expensive if you didn't grow it yourself, and anything that was too expensive we wouldn't eat. But we really liked asparagus, so my dad had to grow it in our garden.

We were all pretty close in our neighborhoods, even to people we weren't actually related to. Maybe sometimes people took that too far. Like this one day when a lady from the neighborhood came into our yard with a shopping bag and started picking things from our garden. It was pretty strange watching her out there, so I called to her (in Italian): "What are you doing out there?"

And she answered (in Italian): "I'm just picking a few things."

I was all for sharing with people, but I was a little annoyed watching her out there picking away at all our hard work. "Why didn't you just ask me?" I called. "I'da given them to you." And I would have. I just didn't want her to think it was okay for her to come around and just take what she wanted. Even if she was family, that wouldn't be okay.

Anyway, we really liked asparagus and had it a lot. And you'd never guess it, but it actually makes for a pretty tasty sandwich. You can toast the bread but you don't have to. Here's how to prepare it.

You will need

20 stalks asparagus
2 teaspoons olive oil
Salt and pepper
8 slices fresh bread, thickly sliced

1. Preheat the oven to 350°F.

2. Place the asparagus in a single layer on a baking sheet. Drizzle the oil evenly over the asparagus, and sprinkle with salt and pepper to taste. Or, lightly roll the oiled asparagus in salt and pepper to fully coat.

3. Roast for about 15 minutes, so that they soften but still have some firmness to them.

4. Fill each sandwich with 5 stalks of asparagus. Serve and enjoy.

Salad Sandwich

I'LL NEVER FORGET how hard it was when I started first grade and I didn't speak a lick of English. Luckily, my cousin Mary was in my class and she spoke both Italian and English. This would have been great except we didn't sit close to each other. My teacher wanted me to sit up front; I guess she thought I'd learn faster like that. But I wanted

to sit next to Mary. So I'd get up a lot and go to Mary's desk, which made the teacher, who was a nun, pretty mad. "Clara, go sit in your own seat!" she'd holler. So I'd go back to my seat.

I was *always* in trouble. Mary was the "good one," so good she later became a nun.

The sister would start talking again, and pretty soon I couldn't understand what she was saying and I would go back to where Mary was again to ask her what the teacher was saying. And then the nun would holler at me again. "Clara, go back to your seat!"

"But I can't understand what you're saying," I'd say back, with tears in my eyes.

"Well, you'd better start understanding!" she snapped. She was real strict.

That first year was bad, it was hard for me that I couldn't understand anything. Second and third grades were much better. The teacher would say something and I'd understand and I'd say to myself, "Oh, thank God, I understood that."

With a lot of thanks to Mary, I finally got the hang of it. Except for one day when I couldn't figure out how to ask: "Sister, may I go to the bathroom?" And Mary wasn't there so she couldn't help me. So I ended up peeing on the floor.

"Why didn't you say you had to go to the bathroom!"

Luckily I lived right across the street from the elementary school, so I could run home if something as bad as this happened. I always knew that Ma would fix me up and maybe fix up one of my favorite sandwiches. When she didn't have anything else, Ma would make sandwiches with either spinach or escarole. It was very simple, but very healthy.

You will need

6 cups spinach or escarole
Olive oil
Salt and pepper
8 slices bread, thickly sliced and toasted

1. Wash the leaves and boil them for 3 to 5 minutes, or until tender.

2. Drain, cool, and squeeze out all the excess water.

3. Toss the greens with olive oil and salt and pepper to taste, and place between the bread slices. And that's it.

Stale Ham Sandwich

• Serves 1 (or in our case, 3) •

M Y MOTHER MADE ME and Sam sandwiches with all kinds of things inside, but meat was always such a commodity, we never had it in any of our sandwiches. Not even hot dogs. Not for lunch. But my father was a different story. My mother always slipped fresh, unprocessed ham into his sandwich, which she would buy at one of my uncle's grocery stores. They used to slice it just like they do now. It was never a thick cut, but it was real ham, not processed at all. Sometimes he felt so guilty about it, though, he'd only eat half and bring the other half home for us kids. We couldn't wait for him to get home from work so we could get a taste of that Stale Ham Sandwich of his.

Remember, we didn't have things like Ziploc bags or Tupperware, so that sandwich was out all day long. Of course, it was terrible and hard to eat, but it was our favorite because it was from Dad.

You will need

2 slices bread

1 tablespoon butter

1 to 2 slices unprocessed ham

A handful of cooked dandelions if in season (see page 36),
or 1 piece regular lettuce if not

1. Butter both slices of bread and place the ham and vegetables between the slices. You might also decide to spread butter on top.

2. Slice into two halves and eat half now.

3. Leave the other half out on the kitchen counter for a few hours, and enjoy it stale when you come back to it. I like my food tough, but never eat something if it's spoiled.

Caprese on Fresh Bread

*C*aprese is a traditional Italian salad that is usually made with fresh mozzarella cheese, ripe tomatoes, and fresh basil leaves. You can make it with regular mozzarella and you can sprinkle it with dry herbs, but fresh cheese and herbs are best if you have them. You can even make it with sun-dried tomatoes, which we used to do from time to time.

Sun-dried tomatoes aren't hard to make. They just take time. Most people make sun-dried tomatoes just like you think: by drying out tomatoes in the sun for a few days. But not Ma. She liked to dry out those tomatoes in the oven because, for one, the sun took too long, but more important, it was too dirty outside. If she could have grown the entire garden inside, she would have. For the vegetables and all the herbs we grew, like bay leaves, rosemary, basil, she'd try and cover everything with nets to keep the bugs off.

My ma used to make Caprese as a sandwich, I guess so she could make it a meal instead of just a salad. She'd make it open-faced, and like a bruschetta in that she'd chop everything up to make it easier to eat on the bread.

You will need

    4 large ripe tomatoes, roughly sliced

    1 pound fresh mozzarella cheese, sliced

    2 cloves garlic, minced

    3 tablespoons extra-virgin olive oil

    ⅓ cup fresh basil leaves

    Salt and pepper

    8 slices fresh Italian bread, thickly sliced
        and lightly toasted

1. Lay out the slices of tomato and cheese on a platter, overlapping the slices. Sprinkle with garlic and drizzle with olive oil. Top with basil and salt and pepper to taste.

2. Serve with the toasted bread.

Eggplant Burgers

YOU ALREADY KNOW we rarely ever had meat, but you may not know how creative we got with substitutes— like when we really wanted a hamburger. All we did was cut open an eggplant. And we'd make it with all the trimmings too. Homemade ketchup and pickles really made us feel like we were having real burgers. Sometimes today I even prefer Eggplant Burgers to the real thing. Using eggplant instead of beef is a good way to save money and eat healthy.

You will need

> 4 to 8 large eggplant slices, about ½ inch thick
>
> 4 tablespoons vegetable oil
>
> 8 slices fresh Italian bread
>
> 4 leaves of escarole, romaine, or other lettuce
>
> Ketchup (recipe follows), mustard, mayo, or whatever you like on a burger, if desired
>
> 4 Quick Pickles (recipe follows)

Take It from Me

If you're just looking to fry something up, like here, save your olive oil and use less expensive vegetable oil instead.

1. If desired, salt the eggplant slices, let stand for an hour, rinse, then pat dry. Pour the vegetable oil into a large frying pan and set over medium-high heat.

2. When the oil begins to shimmer, add one or two slices of the eggplant. If the oil becomes too hot, lower the heat to medium or medium-low.

3. Carefully flip the slices every couple of minutes. They should become brown on the edges after about 5 to 7 minutes.

4. Remove the slices from the pan and place them on a plate lined with paper towel to absorb the extra oil. Repeat until all the slices are cooked.

5. Put one or two slices of eggplant between two slices of bread. Add a leaf of escarole to each sandwich and your favorite condiment, if desired. Serve with a Quick Pickle on the side.

Quick Pickles

WHAT WENT GREAT with these burgers were the homemade pickles Ma made and jarred so we could have them all year long. But when cucumbers were in season she would make us these Quick Pickles so we could have them the next day instead of waiting over a month to taste them.

You will need

3 to 6 small cucumbers

3 cups water

2 tablespoons salt

2 cups sugar

3 cloves garlic, minced

2 cups distilled white vinegar

1 teaspoon mustard seeds

1. Pour the water, salt, and ¾ cup of the sugar into a sterilized jar, and stir until the salt and sugar dissolve. Add the garlic and then the cucumbers. (Make sure the cucumbers aren't waxed or thick-skinned, as these won't be able to absorb the mixture very well.)

2. Put a lid on the jar and refrigerate for 2 to 3 hours. Remove the jar from refrigerator and strain the cucumbers. Rinse well to remove the salt and strain again.

3. Pour the vinegar into a saucepan and bring to a boil. Add the remaining sugar plus the mustard seeds to the vinegar.

4. Place the cucumbers into the boiling vinegar mixture and remove just before they return to a boil. Transfer to the sterile container with enough of the vinegar mixture to cover them. Seal and chill in the refrigerator or eat them warm.

Homemade Ketchup

And what's a burger without ketchup?

You will need

> 6 ounces tomato paste (homemade or canned)
>
> ¼ cup water
>
> 1 clove garlic, pressed
>
> 2 tablespoons vinegar
>
> ½ teaspoon salt

Mix all the ingredients together and put in a sterilized jar. Keep refrigerated.

Panecotto (Cooked Bread)

WE NEVER THREW ANYTHING AWAY. We had to hold on to everything as long as possible. We never got a "free lunch." Even though my two uncles owned grocery stores, they never gave us a break until the food was about to go bad. Then they'd cut the price. And that was fine with us.

We could make anything new again. When bananas went black, we'd buy up the bunch. They were really cheap that way, and usually they were only black on the outside. On the inside, they were ripe and delicious.

No, we never threw anything away. We were healthy. We were happy. Even before the Depression, we held on to things. If you could cut off and save even an inch of food from something that looked like it was rotten, or on its way to rotten, you did it. Kids today will throw away anything. They just don't know better.

Some people may say stale bread is for the birds, but we ate it. You just had to know how to bring it back to life. This recipe for *panecotto*, or cooked bread, proves it. You can make this when your bread is hard and there isn't anything else you think you can do with it. Believe it or not, it makes a very nice meal. Healthy, good for you, and delicious. And it's very good for young children and old people that don't have their teeth anymore. It goes down real easy. I still have all my own teeth, but I know most people around my age don't anymore.

Take It from Me

Panecotto is fine with water, but if you want to give yourself a treat, and you can spare it, use milk.

You will need

1 cup water (or 1 cup milk)
2 thick slices stale bread
1½ tablespoons olive oil
¼ teaspoon salt

1. Heat the water or milk on the stove and carefully cut the stale bread into chunks.

2. When the liquid boils, pour it evenly over the bread. Drizzle the olive oil over the bread and mash it all up with a fork. Add a little more water if it doesn't mash completely. Season with salt and serve.

CHAPTER THREE

It's a Hot Meal— Stop Complaining

M Y MOTHER HAD A SAYING: *"O' di mangi sta minestra, o' di butto da finestra."* Roughly translated, it means: "Eat this mush, or I'll throw you out on your tush." Actually, my mother had a lot of interesting sayings.

I grew up thinking that my mother only spoke Italian. It wasn't until after I was married that I discovered that I was wrong. My sister-in-law came over to the States from Italy. I introduced her to my mother and let them converse. When I checked in, my sister-in-law looked at me with surprise. "Your mother doesn't speak Italian!" she said. My mother thought she was speaking perfect Italian, but she would be speaking some Italian, some Italian-English, and throw in Sicilian to fill in the blanks. Ital-ish. Here are some of my favorites:

o'crewbo sto-ne: street curb
pucho: porch

streeto: street
yarda: yard

However she referred to it, dinner in my day wasn't something you caught on your way to something else. It was a time for the whole family to come together. It was when we caught up with each other's lives, talked about school, and, later, made the plans we needed to dedicate ourselves to and carry out so we could survive. And no matter what was served, we were expected to eat it. At least my mother was a good cook, so even if she made something terrible, you could still choke it down. Not everyone was that lucky.

The Poorman's Meal

· Serves 4 ·

PEOPLE DON'T REALIZE how easy they have it these days. Most kids have never known what it's like to go without anything. They want something, they get it. If there isn't enough money, then charge it. We never wanted anything because we never realized we could have anything. We never missed what we never had. Things were much simpler back then, and we were stronger for it. We worked together to keep the house in order, to put food on the table. We kept things going.

But one thing that is the same between then and now is that even kids today like the Poorman's Meal. My grandson, Mark, likes it. His friends all like it. They all come here for a Poorman's Meal. Even the neighborhood kids come over. "Can we have the Poorman's Meal?" they ask me. What's not to like? Potatoes, onions, hot dogs. We ate plenty of hot dogs because they were cheaper than other meats. Cheap,

easy, and satisfying—that's the Poorman's Meal. Here's how to make it.

You will need

> 4 tablespoons vegetable oil
> 3 large potatoes, peeled and cubed
> 1 onion, sliced
> Water, as needed
> 4 hot dogs, sliced into rounds
> 3 tablespoons tomato sauce
> Pecorino Romano cheese, optional

1. Pour the oil into a frying pan and place over medium heat. Add the potatoes and onions and let the potatoes brown slowly, stirring occasionally.

2. Pour in a little water to help soften the potatoes and to keep them from sticking to the pan.

3. When the potatoes are crisp and golden brown on all sides, add the hot dogs and let simmer about 3 minutes, or until they begin to curl. Add the tomato sauce and turn off the heat. Let the meal cook in its own heat for about 5 more minutes.

4. Serve immediately, topped with Pecorino Romano cheese, if desired.

Take It from Me

If you run out of oil, just add a little water to your pan. It will keep food from sticking—and it's free.

Egg Drop Soup

WE MADE A lot of things with eggs, but unlike people today, we never had them at breakfast. We really didn't eat much at breakfast, maybe just a slice of bread with butter and coffee. We didn't really have much at dinner, either. But that's the way it was. Times were tough for everyone, and everyone was on edge. Adults were worried about feeding their kids and keeping their homes. Kids were sad because their parents were always on edge. There was no special treatment for boys or girls. We all had to pitch in and do our share.

Sometimes we went on vacations together as a big family. It was cheaper that way. We'd rent a house together and keep expenses low. If we went to a resort, we'd always prepare our own meals in our lodgings. We'd also share all the time if anyone wanted to eat with us.

I remember one year we went to Lake Geneva for a vacation, and there was this girl there that my cousins and I became friends with. She would eat with us and then she'd go to the restaurant and eat again. She said we never fed her enough. One day, we found her in the restaurant eating after we'd just had dinner, and we were shocked. "We just got through eating!" I said. To which she replied, "I'm sorry, but you guys don't eat that much and I'm ashamed to eat in front of you." Yeah, she was nice and chunky. We were all pretty bony but healthy. I wonder whatever happened to her?

Anyway, when we were all together, my mother and my aunts would always make something simple they could stretch out to serve lots of hungry mouths. This soup was pretty popular on those nights. It's inexpensive, nutritious, and delicious with fresh bread.

You will need

    1 large potato, cubed
    1 onion, diced
    1 bay leaf, dried and crumbled
    3 tablespoons olive oil
    8 large eggs
    Salt and pepper
    Pecorino Romano cheese

1. In a saucepan, add the potato, onion, crumbled bay leaf, and olive oil. Set over medium heat and let the vegetables brown.

2. Crack four of the eight eggs into a bowl and whisk them. Set aside. Keep the other four eggs whole.

3. Once the potatoes are nice and brown, add water to the pot to about the halfway mark to make the broth. Simmer and add salt and pepper to taste.

4. When the water boils, pour in the whisked eggs. Now carefully crack the other four directly into the pot, without whisking them, and try and keep them whole.

5. Add the Pecorino Romano cheese and stir. Turn off the heat and keep the pot covered to finish cooking until you're ready to eat. Each person should get one whole egg when you serve the soup.

Drunken Chuck's Minestrone

• **Serves 6 to 8** •

WE MADE OUR OWN WINE during the Depression, so there was always plenty of it. At first we'd stomp grapes, but eventually Dad got a machine. We all drank wine. Even the kids got to drink wine with dinner from an early age. It was watered down a lot, but we got to have it.

Everyone in the neighborhood would buy grapes by the crate, and everyone would get their delivery at the same time. We'd get a delivery of 150 boxes of grapes to make maybe one or two barrels of wine. But it was precious to my parents and my uncles and aunts. (We'd give up our stockings, but we had to have our wine.) I learned just how precious this wine was to my parents the hard way when I was about ten or twelve years old and I left the spigot open when I was filling the jug for dinner. Man, did I ever get a lickin' that night.

I had an uncle, Charles, who used to drink wine all day long, from morning to night. He owned a grocery store, which was in the front of his house, but working never stopped him from drinking. He'd just help a customer when they came in and then go right back to his wine. He'd fill a giant gallon jug in the morning, and by dinner, he had it finished.

He didn't get into any trouble, drunk all day like that. He just sat there and stewed, getting mad at my aunt Rose— my father's sister. She was very calm with him. Mostly he was a happy-go-lucky drunk, and a lot of the ladies in the neighborhood used to like to come into his store. And lots of people in the town took phone calls at the store, because no one had phones in their houses.

The most annoying thing he used to do was to "fix" my aunt's minestrone as she cooked it over the course of the day. Every time he got up, he'd dump something else in there. And she was so calm about it all. Even though he changed the soup so much, she never knew it was hers anymore. We called it Drunken Chuck's Minestrone. Here's a variation of it that actually starts out with the vegetables instead of throwing them in when you feel like it. Of course, you can do that, too, if that's what you want to do.

You will need

> 3 tablespoons olive oil
> 1 leek, sliced crosswise
> 2 carrots, chopped
> 1 zucchini, thinly sliced
> 2 celery stalks, thinly sliced
> 1½ quarts vegetable stock
> 1 pound tomatoes, chopped
> 1 can cannellini beans, drained and rinsed
> ¼ cup dry elbow macaroni, or pasta of your choice
> Salt and pepper

1. Heat the olive oil in a large saucepan over medium heat. Add the vegetables and cover. Reduce the heat to low, and cook about 15 to 20 minutes, stirring occasionally.

2. Stir in the stock and tomatoes and bring to a boil. Cover again (to make sure no one else slips anything else in without you knowing about it), reduce the heat to low, and simmer for 30 minutes.

3. Stir in the cannellini beans and the macaroni and simmer an additional 10 minutes, or until the pasta is cooked. Season with salt and pepper to taste before serving.

Twice-Baked Potatoes

W E REALLY NEVER, never threw anything away. You think you know about recycling? We invented it. We had to. We were desperate. Sometimes maybe the only thing we had to work with was a couple of leftover baked potatoes from the weekend, and that was all there was to eat. Didn't matter to us that much. Ma just baked them again. Twice-Baked Potatoes really were kind of a treat for us, and we'd never complain when she served them. I still make these as a treat for the family during the holidays. They may sound fancy but they're actually pretty simple. There's nothing like a good baked potato.

In case you don't have some old baked potatoes lying around, waiting to go in the trash, we'll start from the beginning, actually baking the potatoes first.

You will need

    6 uncooked, scrubbed baking potatoes or
        6 leftover baked potatoes
    8 tablespoons (1 stick) butter
    1 teaspoon salt
    Paprika

1. Preheat the oven to 375° F.

2. Wash and dry the potatoes. Rub approximately 2 tablespoons of the butter over the skins.

3. Put the potatoes on a baking sheet and let bake for about 1½ hours. Stick the potatoes with a fork. If it goes in easily, they're done. Let cool for about 20 minutes. (Now here's where you'd start with those old potatoes.)

4. Carefully remove the top third of the potato with a knife. Scrape the potato pulp off the skin of the potato tops and save it in a medium bowl. Scoop the rest of the potato pulp into the bowl, being careful not to break the potato skins. Put the potato skins aside.

5. While the potatoes are still warm, add the remaining 6 tablespoons of butter and the salt, and mash the potatoes with a fork. When properly mashed, fill the skins, dividing the mixture evenly. Sprinkle a little paprika on each stuffed potato.

6. Set the oven to broil. Broil the potatoes for about 10 minutes, or until the tops are a golden brown color. Serve and enjoy.

Giuseppe of Arabia Couscous

M Y FATHER WAS SICILIAN, through and through, but he grew up in Northern Africa. He was only six years old when his parents, Salvatore and Clara, moved their family to Tunis, Africa, where Salvatore had found work as an orchard keeper at the family estate of a wealthy landowner.

Already having a mind of his own, my dad told his mother that he didn't want to attend school in Tunis, so at the young age of six, she sent him away to learn a trade.

They brought him to a blacksmith and he worked under the blacksmith and eventually became one himself, a trade he worked in until he was twenty-three and they left Tunis for the United States.

He never forgot his experience over there. He talked about those days a lot and my mother knew how much that part of his life meant to him. So my mother learned to make couscous for him. And every time she surprised him with it, he'd perk right up, no matter how hard his day was. To make this she would wrap up the pot with a cloth, just like a real Arab. On those nights he was the happiest man in the world.

You will need

4 cups water

One 10.5-ounce can chicken broth

2 small turnips, chopped

2 carrots, chopped

2 celery stalks (with leaves) chopped

½ potato, cubed

1 whole small onion, finely chopped

One 10-ounce package plain couscous

2 to 3 tablespoons butter

1 small bunch parsley, about 6 sprigs

1. In a large pot, bring the water and broth to a boil. Add the vegetables, and continue boiling over medium heat for 15 minutes, or until the vegetables are tender.

2. Put a colander in the pot and line it with a thin, damp cloth. Put the couscous in the colander over the damp cloth.

Take another damp cloth—use a larger one this time, cheesecloth if you have it—and wrap it over both the colander and pot. (Be careful that it doesn't cover the handles of the pot.)

3. Top everything with the pot's lid. Be extremely careful when opening to check the progress, there will be very hot steam.

4. After about 30 minutes, stir in 1 to 1½ tablespoons of the butter. Make sure it is evenly melted in the couscous. Cover again.

5. After the broth has been cooking for about 1½ hours, remove the colander, add another 2 to 3 cups of water to the broth, stir, re-cover the couscous, and replace the lid. Continue cooking.

6. After 2 more hours, add another 1 to 1½ tablespoons of the butter, and let it melt evenly in the couscous. Cover again and continue cooking for another 45 minutes, adding a little more water to the broth if necessary. Serve the couscous warm, with the vegetables on top.

While the Water Boils . . .
Egyptian (Pyramid) Solitaire

I thank God for letting me keep my mind in my old age. I like to keep my brain sharp and active even when I am alone. I keep books of puzzles in the kitchen and by my favorite recliner, and at the kitchen table I always have a deck of cards to play Solitaire.

I play all types of Solitaire, but the one I play the most is Egyptian Solitaire. It's not really from Egypt, but you deal the cards in a pyramid just like the pharaohs' tombs. It's easy to play, and the game goes fast. It's also very fun to play—unless you're on a losing streak.

The goal: To eliminate all cards from the pyramid.

You will need
1 deck of cards, with the face cards removed
  (40 cards total)

Shuffle the deck and deal the cards into a pyramid, one card, then two under the first card, and three under the second two, and so on, until the last row has 7 cards. The bottom row is considered "open" since there are no cards touching the bottom or "locking" them in. Keep the rest of the deck intact.

Clear all the cards from the pyramid, clearing only cards that are "open." To clear open cards the sum of the numbers on two open cards needs to be 10. For example, if a seven and three are open, you can remove them from the pyramid. The same goes for a nine and an ace (which has a value of one), or an eight and a two, a six and a four, and a five and a five. You may only add the sums of two cards, so adding 2 twos and a six is not allowed. If you have an open ten, you can remove it without the combination of another card.

In the process of removing open cards, you may free previously "locked" cards. If these cards no longer have a card attached to their bottoms, you can now combine them with another open card, and if they add up to ten, you can remove them.

Once you have removed all of the possible tens, take the remaining deck and turn over the cards, one at a time. If a card can be combined with one of the pyramid's open cards to make ten, then you may remove the cards and put them in the discard pile. Repeat this until you run out of cards or, if you clear the pyramid, you win.

CHAPTER FOUR

Pasta . . . Again

WE NEVER HAD a lot of money, but there was a time when my dad was working at a good job and we had everything we needed. We didn't want anything past that. We didn't know we could. My parents always raised us to get by with less than what we had or could afford and to work hard to preserve what we had—our clothes, our shoes, whatever it was. So when the Depression hit, we didn't realize how bad it was right away. A lot of kids didn't. They'd maybe notice that the few special treats they were used to went away ("I can't have chocolate anymore"), but it was the parents who felt it the hardest—at least at first.

That's just how it was in my house in the beginning. My parents might be a little sad about things. Maybe they would fight a little more, be frustrated over money. After a few years, things got bad enough that we noticed. Or maybe we just got old enough to notice.

The Di Maria Family Sauce

· Makes 5 cups ·

I LOVED SCHOOL. I took after my dad that way. I really liked all my subjects and looked forward to learning. It wasn't like there was any place to go after school. Most people didn't go to college in those days, and lots of kids were lucky if they got to finish at all.

School wasn't like it is today. We had one teacher, a nun, who taught us everything. And there were so many of us in one classroom—sixty, seventy kids. So they took some of the girls who were supposed to be smarter than the other kids and put them in their own class with no teacher. Just the girls reading the books and working it out together. We

had no one teaching us or supervising us. There weren't enough teachers. But we still managed to learn things, and it really made me happy.

So the day I found out I had to stop going . . . I think that's the day I realized how bad things really were. My mother just said to me one morning: "You can't go to school anymore." At first she meant this because I was down to one dress that I washed so much it was almost just threads, and they couldn't afford another one for me. And the stockings I had had so many holes in them, they weren't keeping me warm anymore, and sometimes my legs would be soaking wet from walking home in the snow. But later, I realized it was because we were going to lose the house if someone didn't help bring in some money to pay the taxes. And that someone had to be me.

No matter how little we had, we never felt hungry. We ate a lot of pasta and it filled our bellies. Pasta is cheap and filling. What more can you ask for? We had pasta almost every night during the week, but on Thursdays, it was pasta with the famous Di Maria Family Sauce. Sometimes on Thursdays, we also had meat. We didn't have a lot of it, but we sometimes had it.

Take It from Me

If you're adding meat to your sauce, don't add olive oil or basil. There will be enough oil from the meat, and you shouldn't eat basil with meat. Use a stalk of fresh rosemary instead.

You will need

> 2 tablespoons olive oil
> 6 ounces tomato paste, homemade or canned
> 40 ounces canned, diced tomatoes, or 5 cups fresh
>   tomatoes, peeled and diced
> 1 large unpeeled clove garlic
> 2 dried bay leaves
> 2 fresh basil leaves

1. Put the olive oil, tomato paste, and diced tomatoes in a large pot. Place over medium-high heat.

2. Add the clove of garlic whole, skin and all. Next add the bay leaves. When the sauce begins to boil, lower the heat to medium-low and add the fresh basil.

3. Simmer for about 1 hour. (If you decide to add meat to the sauce, you can cook it longer, by another 30 minutes or so.)

4. Before serving, remove the garlic and bay leaves. Freeze any unused sauce for future meals.

Take It from Me

Leave the whole clove of garlic intact in the sauce until the end of the cooking. This will give you all the flavor of the garlic, and it's easy to remove it before serving the sauce.

Pasta with Garlic and Oil

· **Serves 4 to 6** ·

SOMETIMES WE HAD SPECIAL PASTA, like on Thursdays, when we had it with the Di Maria Family Sauce (see page 94), which had been handed down in my mother's family for generations. Sometimes we had it with a few ingredients, like Pasta with Peas (see page 110) and some of the recipes you'll find in the rest of this chapter. But if my mom wasn't doing the cooking, it was anyone's guess what we'd end up with.

For instance, when my dad was left in charge of us, he didn't know what to do about feeding us. He had no idea how to cook anything, so he just made us Pasta with Butter—even though butter was expensive. He wouldn't add anything else to it. He'd just cook up the pasta, cut up some butter, and toss it with the pasta until it melted. That was that.

Sometimes we'd share food with the upstairs tenants, and they'd share food with us. But I think we got the raw end of the deal there. They'd make Pasta with Lard, which I didn't like at all. Basically, all they did was to cut up chunks of lard and toss it with the cooked pasta. Lard doesn't melt as well (or taste as good) as butter. Actually, Pasta with Lard was disgusting, but we had to choke it down because if we didn't eat that, we didn't eat.

When I got older, I learned it didn't take much effort or skill to make pasta special, even if you had nothing to put in it, and that you could still do it on the cheap and with barely any ingredients but still make it memorable (in a good way). I started making Pasta with Garlic and Oil and it was delicious—and not more complicated than my dad's or aunt's dishes. It was so good, it's still my favorite. I still make it for myself sometimes. I used to use my small pot without the handle to make this. I really loved that pot, but it started getting dangerous lifting it off the hot stove with pliers, so I had to throw it away. I hate to throw things away.

You will need

> 1 pound dry pasta (of your choice)
> ¼ cup olive oil
> 3 cloves garlic, minced

Take It from Me

Use a small frying pan to fry up the garlic. It will heat the garlic evenly and also prevent the oil from splashing around.

1. Boil water and cook the pasta. (Follow the directions on the box to find out how long—anywhere from 5 to 13 minutes.)

2. While the pasta is cooking, heat the oil in a frying pan. When it's hot, toss in the garlic. Sauté until the garlic is nice and brown.

3. Drain the pasta and pour it into a large bowl with the olive oil and garlic. Toss a few times to get all the pasta coated, and then serve.

Pasta with Beans (Pasta Fagioli)

Serves 4 to 6

BETWEEN YOU AND ME, I used to hate eating Pasta with Beans, but that's because we had to eat it so much. Over the years, I've started to like it more. I remember in my house growing up, there were lots of things I didn't like to eat that my mother made me eat. And then there were lots of things my own family didn't like to eat. But I made them anyway. I guess that's just how it goes.

We had Pasta with Beans almost every week, sometimes twice or three times a week. Usually my mom would just make it with pasta, beans, garlic, and olive oil, but every so often she would make a real Pasta Fagioli. And that would be really special.

You will need

> 5 tablespoons olive oil
>
> 1 clove garlic, thinly sliced
>
> 1 yellow onion, thinly sliced
>
> 2 cups of tomato sauce (see the Di Maria Family Sauce, page 94)
>
> 3½ cups water
>
> 1 carrot, chopped
>
> 1 celery stalk (with leaves), chopped

1 cup dried cannellini beans (white kidney beans),
  or 2 cups canned
2 chicken bouillon cubes
1 large fresh basil leaf
2 dried red peperoncini, crushed
1 pound small dry pasta
  (such as ditalini or mini shells)
¼ cup chopped flat-leaf parsley
Pecorino Romano cheese

Take It from Me

If you decide to use dried beans, rinse them well before cooking. Add 1 cup dried cannellini beans to 6 cups boiling water and boil rapidly for 3 minutes. Remove from heat and cover. Soak overnight. This makes about 2 cups. Before you begin the recipe, cook the presoaked beans by boiling them in water with a pinch of salt for about 10 minutes. Lower the heat, cover, and simmer for an additional hour.

1. Put the olive oil into a large pot set over medium-high heat. Add the garlic and onion and cook until caramelized, 5 to 7 minutes.

2. Add the tomato sauce, water, carrots, celery, cannellini beans, bouillon cubes, basil leaf, and peperoncini. Cover, venting slightly, and cook over medium heat, stirring occasionally, until the sauce is reduced, about 35 minutes.

3. While the sauce is reducing, cook the pasta until al dente (about 2 minutes less than what the directions on the box say, or approximately 7 minutes).

4. Strain the pasta and pour it into the sauce. Turn off the heat and stir for 2 minutes. Top with chopped fresh parsley and Pecorino Romano cheese and serve.

Pasta with Escarole

A NOTHER JOB I had was at the Hostess Twinkie factory. I worked there a while and only quit because it was so far away from my house and I used to walk most of the time. It was five miles both ways and it took forever. So sometimes I'd beg my cousin, Tony Lapi, for his skates. And, as usual, most of the time he'd let me. That made the trip faster, but not fast enough.

But making the Twinkies was a fun job. I started right on the factory floor, and it was just like that scene in *I Love Lucy*, where Lucy and Ethel are working at the chocolate factory, and the candies are coming out much too fast for them to process and they end up stuffing them in their mouths and their clothes and anywhere they can find. It seems like it could have been stressful but it was actually a lot of fun. And I guess eventually I got good at it because I was promoted to the coveted "Twinkie Puncher" position.

This was the last factory job I ever held, though. After Hostess, I got a job in the Richardson Factory, where I started out on the floor but then ended up in the back office. I stayed at that job doing clerical work for the next twenty years.

But whether I was making that long commute from the Hostess factory or not, I was pretty wiped out when I got home, and Ma knew exactly how to give me some of my pep

back: with a nice big bowl of pasta with some high-energy vegetable in it, like this recipe for Pasta with Escarole. By the next morning, I was all revved up and ready to go. (Or roll, if I got lucky and got the skates that day.)

You will need

1 head escarole
1 pound pastina (or mini shells, ditalini, or angel hair)
¼ cup olive oil
Salt and pepper
Pecorino Romano cheese, optional

1. Rinse the escarole and chop it into small pieces. Boil the escarole in a large pot of water with a dash of salt for 3 to 5 minutes, or until wilted and tender.

2. Boil the pasta in a separate pot until al dente (follow the directions on the package), and drain.

3. Drain the escarole, reserving ¼ cup of the cooking water, and toss it with the pasta, along with the oil and salt and pepper to taste. Top with the cheese and serve.

Take It from Me

Walk when you go to the grocery store. Because if you don't have a large car trunk to store things, you'll be forced to buy only what you can comfortably carry, which is most likely all you need.

Pasta with Broccoli

W E NEVER HAD ANYTHING, and we'd borrow lots of things from my cousins. They were usually nice about it but sometimes they would torture us. I would just die for a pair of skates. My cousin Tony Lapi had a pair of skates and I wanted to skate so badly that I'd beg him to let me borrow his skates. I'd ask him over and over until he finally said, "If you can find them and fix them up, then you can use them."

All the parts of his skates were in different places; they were real dilapidated so I would have to take pieces of string and tie them back together. And by the time I got them all ready it would be time to go home. But he would let me take them home and fix them up so I could go skating the next day. He was a nice boy really.

Once they were all patched up I would finally take them out. There was just one block in the neighborhood that had a paved road, it was where the Germans lived, and all of the kids would be there skating up and down the street. Of course my mom got mad about this. She didn't want me going up and down the street. But when I got home, she would still have a nice meal for me, like Pasta with Broccoli.

You will need

16 ounces fresh broccoli, chopped
1 pound dry angel hair pasta
¼ cup olive oil
Salt and pepper
Pecorino Romano cheese

1. Bring water to a boil in two large pots: one for the broccoli, one for the pasta.

2. Add the broccoli to one pot and cook for 9 to 10 minutes, or until it's tender enough that you can pierce it with a fork. Drain and set aside.

3. Boil the pasta for about 4 minutes in the second pot. Drain, leaving about ¾ cup of the cooking water at the bottom of the pot.

4. Toss the pasta and broccoli together in the pasta pot with the cooking water. Add the olive oil, salt and pepper, and cheese to taste. Serve and enjoy.

Take It from Me

Here's a simple way to save time and money: Cook in bulk and freeze leftovers.

Pasta with Swiss Chard

I DIDN'T HAVE A LOT OF SKILLS and there weren't really any jobs, so when it came time for me to quit school and find work, I had to take whatever I could get. And if the job was miserable, so what. It was work. So whenever I didn't like it, I had to do it.

I remember one job I had where I worked in the factory making radio coils. I had a lousy boss there. He was so mean and he never liked me. He used to make fun of me in front of all the girls. It was annoying. And he was always trying to make it look like I was making mistakes. I was getting fed up with all this, and I decided to prove I wasn't messing up all the time like he said I was. So I suggested we mark our coils so if someone made a mistake, we'd know exactly who it was. Well, one day someone made a big mistake. And the boss grabbed that coil and came right up to me.

"See this? See what you did!" he said to me.

I looked at the coil and I looked back at him. "My color's yellow. That one's not mine." And then I went back to work.

But he was so mad, and he got even meaner when he found out it wasn't my mistake. And I was so mad, too, by then, I wished he'd get hit by a train. Well, the very next day, he got hit by a train. He didn't get hurt, just his car really. But I was shocked: "Oh Lord, that was me!"

Working made me much more tired than school, and by the time I was out working, my mother's arthritis had gotten so bad, she really relied on me to help out with dinner, too. After a long day at work, I had to make things that were simple and didn't need that much cleanup. Which is why recipes like this Pasta with Swiss Chard were perfect. Just one pot to clean.

You will need

> 5 big leaves of Swiss chard or 1 head escarole
> ½ pound pennette (mini penne)
> 2 tablespoons olive oil
> Salt and pepper

1. Rinse the Swiss chard and tear the leaves into bite-size pieces. Boil in a large pot of water with a dash of salt for 5 to 7 minutes.

2. Add the pasta to the pot and boil on high until the pasta is al dente, 9 to 10 minutes.

3. Drain pasta, reserving ¼ cup of the cooking water. Toss the pasta and greens with the olive oil, salt and pepper to taste, and the cooking water. Serve hot.

Pasta with Peas

· Serves 4 ·

I'VE BEEN EATING Pasta with Peas since I was a little girl. It's not expensive and it's nourishing. During the Depression we ate a lot of it because about all we ate was pasta. That's about all I can tell you about it. A lot of us worked doing whatever we could to get by during the Depression, and some people found other ways to make money.

I was a kid when Prohibition started and it was scary. It was still going when the Depression started, and the bootleggers would go to every house to try and rent our garages to make whiskey. "We'll build you a new garage if you let us use yours," they'd promise.

One of our neighbors did and that was all we could smell. My father, God rest his soul, said, "I'm not renting my garage to anybody."

My uncle lived next door to us and he didn't rent it either. But the other side, they had barrels of whiskey brewing all the time. The smell of yeast was all over the town.

We made our own wine back then, but it was okay if you made your own. You just couldn't sell it to anyone. We made a lot of things that people don't make anymore these day—like Pasta and Peas. Though I still make it all the time because it's cheap, filling, and nourishing.

You will need

   2 large potatoes, cubed
   1 large yellow onion, diced
   3 tablespoons olive oil
   Two 15-ounce cans peas
   1 pound small-shaped dry pasta (such as ditalini or
      mini shells)
   Salt and pepper
   ¼ cup tomato sauce, optional
   Pecorino Romano cheese, optional

1. Put the potato, onion, and olive oil in a large pot. Set the pot over medium-high heat and sauté the onions and potatoes until they become soft and start to brown, about 10 minutes. Keep an eye on them; you don't want them to burn.

2. When they have a nice golden color, lower the heat and add the peas, liquid and all.

3. Add a cup of warm water. When the mixture begins to boil, add the pasta.

4. Continue cooking for as long as the directions on the pasta box indicate. For the last 2 to 3 minutes, turn off the heat, cover, and let the mixture cook in its own heat.

5. Add salt and pepper to taste. If the sauce seems too plain and you want to give it more flavor, add the tomato sauce. Top with some Pecorino Romano cheese and serve.

Pasta with Beef Scrap Ragu

WHEN I WAS A KID, we always seemed to have a dog. My brother Sam was always bringing animals home, in fact. Sometimes he'd bring home dogs and cats. Sometimes turtles and field mice. Once he even brought home a white rat with a long leathery tail. My mother put up with most of it, but she didn't like that rat one bit. One

day Sam came home from school and the rat was gone. He asked Mom if she knew what happened. "Cat must've got 'im," she said. I don't know if Sam ever knew she was lying. I guess it's better he not know that she got rid of it herself.

Rat, or no rat, we always had a dog. Even in the darkest days of the Depression. I know that probably seems crazy—we were struggling to eat and then we had all these other mouths to feed. But it was easy having pets back then. There wasn't any such thing as pet food. We fed the animals our scraps. There were no pet stores—no one ever bought a pet. They just kind of came to you. And we never took them to the vet. One day they just wouldn't be around anymore.

There was this one dog we had for years. He was our favorite dog, but he used to belong to one of our neighbors. One day, the dog wandered into our yard, and a while later, our neighbor came looking for him. "Gus here?" he'd ask.

"Yep," we'd say. And then Gus would go home with his owner.

And the next day, there was Gus again. And his owner wasn't far behind. "Gus here?" he asked.

And we answered again. "Yep."

The day after that, it was the same. "Gus here?"

And "Yep."

And then the owner looked at us and the dog and then at us again. "Keep 'im," he said, and he just left. I guess we had tastier scraps at our house.

My mother wasn't crazy about all the animals, but she had sense enough to know what people know even today: Pets are good for you. They gave us companionship. They

curled up next to us on cold nights and kept us warm. We gave them scraps and water to live on and they were happy. And we were happy.

Even the garbage got used—to feed the dog. We used scraps from meals for days for us. Until they were too old to eat anymore. Then they went to the dog. But the day before they went to the dog, they were dinner. Beef was vary seldom seen, but after the holidays or festivals we sometimes caught a break. We didn't waste anything. Whatever wasn't eaten immediately would show up the next day in this sauce, like this great meal we used to make from the end of a Roast Beef dinner (see page 148).

You will need

Beef scraps (as much as you are lucky to get)
¼ cup olive oil
⅓ red onion, minced
1 clove garlic, minced
1 carrot, finely chopped
1 sprig fresh rosemary
20 ounces canned tomato sauce, or
    2½ cups fresh tomato sauce
¼ cup red wine
½ pound dry pasta (rigatoni or spaghetti)
Pecorino Romano cheese

1. Cut the scraps of meat into pieces as small as possible, to stretch it out as much as possible.

2. Heat the oil in a frying pan over medium heat. Add the onions and garlic and caramelize until a very light brown, 8 to 10 minutes.

3. Add the finely chopped carrot, beef scraps, and rosemary sprig to the onion and garlic mixture. When the beef is browned, add the tomato sauce and red wine.

4. Lower the heat and simmer for 20 to 30 minutes. Add water if the sauce reduces too much. While the sauce simmers, cook the pasta.

5. Drain the pasta and toss with the ragu. Top with a generous amount of Pecorino Romano cheese and serve.

Handmade Pasta

· **Serves 2 to 4** ·

EVEN TODAY, making homemade pasta by hand is a labor of love. Sure, it tastes the best this way, but it takes so much time and patience. I don't know how my mother ever found enough of either to get it on the table, but she did—not a lot, but it was always special when she did. And it was much cheaper than buying pasta at the store. Here's how she made hers:

You will need

1¼ cups all-purpose flour
2 large eggs
Pinch of salt

1. Add the ingredients to a food processor, or make the dough by hand, first pouring out the flour into a mound on a clean surface and making a well in the center with your fingers. Break the eggs into the well and add the salt.

 With a fork, start working the rest of the flour into the eggs in the center. When the dough becomes too difficult to work with the fork, use your hands to work the rest of the flour into the eggs. Knead the dough for

several minutes, until it has a nice, squishy texture. You may need to add more flour as you go.

2. Cut the dough into six equal pieces and flatten each piece with a rolling pin. Press the dough through your pasta machine, folding each piece in thirds as you roll it through. Keep pressing the dough through the machine until you achieve the desired thickness. After each rolling, lay out the dough on clean towels, making sure the edges don't touch. Rest them on the towels for about 10 minutes, giving them some time to dry out.

3. Pass the dough through the cutter of your pasta machine or cut by hand.

4. Cook the pasta to the desired doneness and toss it with your favorite pasta topping. Just be careful, homemade pasta cooks much faster than dry. You really only need to warm it—probably not more than 3 or 4 minutes at most, depending on the thickness and shape.

No-Potato Gnocchi

· Serves 6 ·

L IKE HANDMADE PASTA, gnocchi is an all-day affair, but it's nice to have once in a while. My mother made it extra-special by not going traditional with it—by leaving out the potatoes and making it with flour instead. I guess she was as sick of potatoes as we were. Anyway, her gnocchi was more like a fresh pasta than a dumpling. Sometimes I wanted to make the gnocchi on my own, but my mother was very particular and always made them herself, but sometimes she let me help. I was never allowed to make them on my own.

When I was older and married with my own family, I once wanted to make my mother's gnocchi for my husband. I did all the work and put it into the water and then walked away. When I came back to the pot the gnocchi had disappeared! They had dissolved into the water. I cried. My husband was coming home from work and I had wanted to surprise him. Well, I did, there was nothing! I had to go back to my mother and convince her to finally share her recipe with me. I guess she felt sorry for me, because here it is.

You will need

8 cups all-purpose flour
2½ cups water
1 tablespoon olive oil
1 teaspoon salt

1. Pour the flour into a large mixing bowl and make a well in the center with your fingers. Slowly add water to the well, ¼ cup at a time. Work the water into the flour with a fork and continue adding water, making the mixture into a smooth dough.

2. Create another well and add the oil and salt. Add a little more water and continue to knead the dough with your hands. Once it is well kneaded, you can start to roll it out.

3. Lightly dust a large surface (I use a wooden table) with flour. Using a knife, cut off a grapefruit-size piece of the dough, and flatten it out with a rolling pin to a thickness of ¼ inch, or thinner.

4. Bring a large pot of lightly salted water to a boil on the stove.

5. When the dough is even, use your knife or an pastry edger to cut out pieces about the size of a postage stamp. Indent each piece with the middle of your thumb. (These days, the best ones are made with the thumbs of my great-grandchildren.)

6. Once all the dough is cut, drop the pieces in the pot and boil until done, 14 to 16 minutes. (You'll know when they're done because they'll float to the top.)

7. Drain and serve with the Di Maria Family Sauce (see page 94) and whatever meat you can find.

While the Water Boils . . .
Crafting Paper Dolls

I remember I got a nurse doll one Christmas, one from World War I. I think I was about six or seven, so Sam was about five. Ma wouldn't let me play with that doll. I was barely allowed to even touch her—maybe only a few minutes at a time. Sam really wanted to play with it, but he was never allowed to touch it even for a minute.

Ma played with it the most. She knew better than to let Sam touch it—it was too precious to risk in the hands of a five-year-old boy. After she'd take it out to let me dress it, brush its hair, and clean and iron its uniform, she would promptly put it away. Sam would look around for it and ask, "Where did it go?" My mother would say, it's with Santa. Since Santa brought the doll, Sam would accept the explanation.

Anyway, my brother started to get pretty jealous that he couldn't play with it, and one day he got so mad he couldn't play with it that he tossed it out the window and it smashed in the street. When my mother came looking for it, Sam said, "I gave it to Santa Claus."

Boy, did he ever get it. My dad never hit us. But my mother . . . I don't know if Sam ever got over the lickin' my mother gave him that day. My mother got that doll fixed somehow and we were never allowed to play with it again. But my mother still played with it all the time.

For me, I had to make do with paper dolls most of the time, at least when I was really young. After a while, I started not caring about dolls at all, when I got into sports. But for the time I was interested in them, paper dolls were a good diversion. Though they'd never top that nurse doll. (And no, I have no idea what ever happened to it.)

These days I have a whole collection of dolls all over my house. Probably about a hundred of them, in all kinds of outfits. I guess this is because I wasn't really ever allowed to play with that nurse doll.

You will need
Pencils, crayons, or markers
Lightweight cardboard
Heavy paper, wallpaper scraps,
    or other materials for clothes
Scissors or X-Acto knife
Scrap yarn or thread, optional
Glue, optional

1. Draw the figure of a doll on a piece of the cardboard and decorate it with a face and hair. Carefully cut it out.

2. Place the doll over the heavy paper, wallpaper scraps, or other materials for clothes, and use as a size guide for drawing the clothes. Be sure that once you've drawn the outfits, you create tabs at the shoulders and sides that you can use to attach the clothes to the doll.

3. Carefully cut around tabs to cut out clothes.

4. If you like, glue scrap yarn or thread to the doll's head to create "hair."

CHAPTER FIVE

A Chicken in Every Other Pot

MEALS WITH ANY kind of meat or fish were rare in my family growing up, and even more so when the Depression hit. But they did happen sometimes, and the idea of them gave us something to look forward to.

Not having meat or fish that much was only one way we saved money when times were tough. We watched every penny, which meant being careful about how much gas we used when we cooked and what kinds of ingredients we cooked with. We didn't have backpacks and we would have to carry our books. Sometimes if we had a lot of books we would have to use a men's belt and strap it around the books. We didn't have electricity until the 1930s, but we conserved the oil in our lamps.

The Saturday meal was the one we looked forward to each week. That's when we'd have a roast chicken or beef or sometimes fish. And the thought of that meal got us through a week, sometimes even a month of potatoes and pasta.

The Poorman's Feast

THE POORMAN'S FEAST was a very special meal during the Depression because we rarely had meat. But sometimes we got lucky and got to have a few bites of steak with our vegetables and rice. This was one of the more luxurious meals we ate, and still it was dirt cheap and very delicious.

If we were sick on a night Ma made the Poorman's Feast, we'd pretend we weren't. It didn't matter how sick we felt. We loved this meal and knew when we had it, we weren't

going to be having it again for a while, so we made sure we didn't miss it, no matter what.

My mother would sometimes make this when she thought we were sick. She thought the lemons were good for making us feel better. So sometimes if we wanted it bad enough, we'd pretend to be sick so she'd make it for us. Then she'd call the doctor, who came to look at us. "There's nothing wrong with you. Get out of bed!"

The Fried Paper-Thin Steak with Lemon and Oil Marinade was a favorite in my house because it was a way to get a "taste" of meat and feel pretty satisfied with it. It goes well with Lentils with Rice and an Endive Salad with Lemon Dressing. The thin steak was cheap, and the lemon and oil marinade made it so soft and tender. We didn't grow lemons in our backyard, but we bought them easily and used them a lot. We could get them three for 25 cents.

This is an easy three-course meal to make. The Lentils with Rice takes the most time to cook, so I usually start preparing that first. I fry the steak and toss the salad while that's cooking, and sometimes I get everything ready at the same time. You can make this on a weeknight pretty easily. It only takes about half an hour or so.

No Poorman's Feast is complete without the bread, so be sure to have a couple of thick slices ready for each person you're feeding to sop up all the delicious flavors. Now you're all set. God bless.

Lentils with Rice

L ENTILS ARE NOT EXPENSIVE and we ate a lot of them. We would have this as a side dish with the Poorman's Feast, but the lentils are so filling and good for you, you could make it as your meal. You could make them with pasta or rice, but I like the rice.

You will need

1 bag lentils
1 teaspoon salt
1 cup white rice

1. Put the full bag of lentils in the pot and add water, according to the directions on the bag. Add salt and set the pot over medium heat and cook until the lentils boil.

2. Add the rice and cover. Simmer until done, 15 to 20 minutes. You can also turn off the heat after about 10 minutes, and let it simmer down by itself.

Take It from Me

When using lentils, be sure you pick through them carefully and remove any stones.

Fried Paper-Thin Steak with Lemon and Oil Marinade

· Serves 4 ·

MY MOTHER HATED FRYING because it made too much grease. She did a lot of it, but she cleaned up the stove even before dinner was on the table. She was such a clean freak, whether it was our house or us that had to be clean. My aunt Lucy fried all the time, but she never cleaned her stove. That made my mother sick. Sometimes she'd sneak off while we were at my aunt's house and clean Lucy's stove. Years

after their husbands had died, someone in the family suggested they move in together. "No way!" my mother said.

You will need

1 cup, plus 2 tablespoons olive oil

Juice of 2 lemons

2 teaspoons salt

2 teaspoons black pepper

4 thin slices steak (You can choose any cut you like, but it has to be cut thin. We didn't know what "thick" meant.)

1. Make two separate marinades by pouring half the olive oil, lemon juice, and salt and pepper into one baking pan, and half into another, and stirring both lightly. Coat both sides of the steak in one of the mixtures and set the other aside. Marinate at least 15 minutes.

2. Heat the remaining 2 tablespoons olive oil in a large frying pan over medium-high to high heat.

3. Fry the steaks for 5 minutes on one side, turn, and fry 3 minutes more on the opposite side. Remove from heat.

4. Rest the hot steaks in the second marinade and let soak for 5 minutes. (We used to use the same marinade as before, but nowadays people tell me you shouldn't do that.)

Take It from Me

Be careful when frying on high heat because the oil spits. I recommend wearing long sleeves and standing back.

Bay Leaf Tea

Here's an old Sicilian remedy right from the garden that takes care of sore throats, stomachaches, and the flu, and one we relied on to help us be well enough to enjoy Ma's Poorman's Feast when we were sick.

You will need

Hot water
2 dried bay leaves
½ teaspoon sugar

Boil the water in a pot with the bay leaves. After it boils, remove from heat and pour it all in a mug, leaves and all. Add the sugar and drink it slowly.

Endive Salad with Lemon Dressing

THE LAST THING we do for the feast is to make the salad, and then your meal is ready to eat. This is a tasty salad that goes well with any meat dish. I like to tear apart the leaves of the salad with my hands, but sometimes I have to use a knife. I also like to toss the salad with my hands. That gives the best coverage of the dressing.

You will need

2 heads endive, carefully washed
¼ cup olive oil
Juice of 1 lemon
Salt and pepper
Dried oregano, optional

1. Carefully tear apart the endive and clean it well. Place it in a bowl.

2. Pour the olive oil over the leaves and squeeze the lemon over the top. Sprinkle with salt and pepper to taste, and a bit of oregano, if you like. Toss and serve.

Take It from Me

Olive oil is a good natural moisturizer. Toss a salad with your hands and you'll see that olive oil works just as well, or even better, than any fancy expensive moisturizer you might be wasting your money on.

Take It from Me

To get the most juice out of your lemons, press on them and roll them around on the countertop before cutting them open, which releases their juices.

The Lonely Meatball

• Serves 4 •

MA HAD A SAYING: *"Mette pane al dente, que appetito si risente."* Which I translate roughly as: "Smell the bread that is baking, and your appetite will reawaken."

Sometimes you don't realize how hungry you are when you don't have a lot to eat, or if what you do have is potatoes again! But once you have food near you that all changes. This was particularly true with my mom's meatballs. We didn't have enough meat for each of us to get our own meatball, but just the little taste of our slice of this lonely meatball made us hungry for the rest of the filler foods in the meal.

This recipe is all about stretching it out and goes great with the Di Maria Family Sauce (see page 94). But if you have a little bit more money this week, double the ingredients, and cut the meatballs in half!

You will need

½ pound ground beef

1 large egg

2 tablespoons bread crumbs

2 tablespoons Pecorino Romano cheese

2 sprigs flat-leaf parsley, chopped

Olive oil

1. Mix all the ingredients, except the olive oil, in a bowl and form into a ball.

2. Lightly coat the meatball with olive oil and drizzle additional oil in a small frying pan set over medium-high heat.

3. Fry the meatball in the oil for approximately 10 minutes, turning it so it browns evenly on all sides.

4. Cut the meatball into quarters and serve.

Take It from Me

They say using olive oil helps you live long. I use lots of it because it makes everything taste better. Even in the Depression my mom would sacrifice everything else before she cut out the olive oil.

One Chicken, Four Meals

One thing about growing up when I did was that we were all pretty strong—we had to be. We didn't have the modern conveniences people have today. We walked just about everywhere we had to go. We washed our clothes by boiling them. (We also used a lot of bleach, which is why I think my bones are so strong.) And then because of my mother's arthritis, we got a washing machine when I was a teenager. It was the best day of my life.

But we still worked hard in so many other ways. Like how we got our food. We all worked in Dad's garden and

picked and cleaned the vegetables when they were ready. We walked to the grocery store, which meant walking all the way back home carrying bags of groceries. And when it was roast chicken night, we chased "dinner" around the yard, slaughtered it, and cleaned it ourselves before we could cook it.

All that extra work we had to do beforehand is what made us so strong and is why I'm so strong today. I can even beat my grandson, Chris, in an arm wrestle. And a few years ago, when I was eighty-eight, I moved the refrigerator by myself. I was getting a new one (after thirty years) and I didn't want the guy to see all the dirt that had built up all that time. I thought he'd mind the dust. So I moved it and I cleaned behind it. And then I moved it back. I didn't want him to know I had moved it, which is why I moved it back like that. I don't think I'm going to move the refrigerator anymore.

Anyway, we didn't have a lot of chickens and needed to keep some around to lay the eggs, so when we did have them, we got as much use out of them as possible. I say here that one chicken can be stretched for four meals, and depending on your family's appetites, maybe that seems like a lot. We did it sometimes, and sometimes one chicken made two meals. It all depended on the week. But even if you start with a new chicken every time, here are four meals that are pretty easy to make and taste good, too.

Day 1. Roast Chicken

· Serves 4 to 6 ·

INVOLVES ONE previously clucking chicken. You can use a whole chicken for roasting, or cut it in half and set aside the other half for *Chicken with Greens* or *Chicken Soup with Pastina*.

You will need

One 4- to 5-pound whole chicken
1 sprig fresh rosemary
1 sprig fresh thyme
2 sprigs flat-leaf parsley
2 tablespoons olive oil
Salt and pepper

Take It from Me

Don't cover the pan when you roast a chicken. Save the aluminum foil. You don't need it here. If you're worried about the breast meat drying out, put it in the oven breast side down, which will keep the meat nice and moist.

1. Preheat the oven to 325°F.

2. Remove all of the guts and the neck from the chicken. Cut out the guts with scissors. The heart, liver, lungs and the gizzard come off whole. The intestines come in a bunch, so you need to unwind them and spread them out in strips. Cut the intestines open along the length of them and, with your fingers, slide out all the waste.

3. Rinse the innards well in water. Soak in a bowl of salted water overnight. Refrigerate until needed on Day 4.

4. Rinse the chicken and pat it dry. Tie the rosemary, thyme, and parsley sprigs together with string. Place the herbs in a dish, then drizzle olive oil over them, and sprinkle them with salt and pepper. Place the herbs inside the chicken. Rub the whole chicken with olive oil and sprinkle it with a thin coat of salt and pepper.

5. Place the chicken on a V-rack, breast side down, and place in the preheated oven. Roast 25 to 30 minutes per pound, or about 2 hours and 20 minutes, basting every 20 minutes or so once the juices start to collect in the pan— after an hour or so. If you have a fancy meat thermometer, it will read 180 degrees when the chicken's done. Of course, the poorman's way is to cut into the thigh; if the juices run clear, it is cooked.

6. Let the chicken rest about 20 minutes before carving. Serve and enjoy.

Day 2. Chicken with Greens

I F YOU CAN AFFORD a whole other chicken, that's great. You only need half of it for this—and you can use the other half for *Chicken Soup with Pastina*.

You will need

½ roasting chicken, about 2 pounds

1 small onion

One 20-ounce jar tomato sauce, or

2½ cups homemade tomato sauce

½ head romaine lettuce

1 tomato

1 cucumber

2 tablespoons olive oil

1 tablespoon lemon juice

Salt and pepper

1. Put the chicken in a large pot and fill the pot with water, enough to submerge the chicken. Bring to a boil. Cover, venting slightly, and boil for 15 to 20 minutes.

2. While the chicken boils, slice and fry half the onion in olive oil until lightly browned. Mix in the tomato sauce.

3. Cut up the lettuce, tomato, cucumber, and remaining onion half. Lightly toss with oil, lemon juice, and salt and pepper to taste.

4. Remove the chicken from the pot. When cool enough to handle, remove the meat from the bones, and divide it into small portions (setting aside and saving the chicken carcass for future broths). Top with tomato sauce, and serve the greens on the side.

Take It from Me

Tomato sauce is nice but in this case it's a luxury. If times are really tight, just forget about the sauce and top the chicken with just the olive oil, lemon juice, and salt and pepper.

Day 3. Chicken Soup with Pastina

W E ATE THIS SOUP a lot if we were sick or my mom made it the day after we killed a chicken. It calls for half a chicken, so you can share the same chicken you killed . . . bought . . . for Chicken with Greens.

You will need

    4 quarts water

    ½ roasting chicken

    3 celery stalks (with leaves), roughly chopped

    4 carrots, roughly chopped

    1 potato, diced

    1 onion, sliced

    6 teaspoons salt

    1 teaspoon pepper

    ½ cup canned peas

    1 cup dry pasta (ditalini or pastina)

1. Bring the water to a boil in a large pot. First, the chicken. I usually pick the bones out of my mouth when I eat the soup, but that's not safe and certainly not good table manners. So to keep the bones from getting into the broth, wrap the half-chicken and chicken bits, bones and all, in a piece of cheese-cloth and secure with a piece of kitchen twine. Add this to the pot, and lower the heat to medium-high.

2. Add the vegetables, except the peas, 5 teaspoons of the salt, and the pepper to the pot. Cover, venting slightly, and simmer at least 90 minutes, or until the liquid has reduced by at least ½ quart.

3. When the broth is done, carefully pull the cheesecloth package out and put it in a colander over a bowl. When it cools, press on the bones lightly to remove as much broth as you can because that will be very flavorful. Add that back to the pan, along with deboned chicken pieces.

4. Bring the broth with the vegetables back to a boil.

5. Add the peas, the pasta, and remaining teaspoon of salt. Cook until the pasta is done, according to the directions on the package.

Day 4. The Rest of the Chicken with Tomato Sauce

· **Serves 4** ·

POOR LITTLE CHICKEN. We ate up every bite of him. Nothing went to waste in our house—even the chicken's head, neck, and guts. Ma would simmer those parts in a pot of tomato sauce and make this simple ragu, which we ate with warm bread. Maybe it sounds icky, but we used to fight over them, they tasted so good. My father always got the head, and my favorite part was the neck.

You will need

All of the reserved chicken innards,
　　plus the neck and head
20 ounces canned tomato sauce or
　　2½ cups homemade sauce
Bread for serving

1. In a pot set over medium heat, bring the sauce to a simmer and, using a slotted spoon, add the reserved innards, plus the neck and head. Bring to a boil.

2. Reduce the heat to low, cover, and simmer for about 1 hour. Serve with bread.

Fried Smelts

WHEN I WAS in high school, we used to have a swimming class right in the middle of the day. I hated it, but I guess that's because I was a little lazy. But we'd have to take off all our clothes, get into our suits, get wet and then get dried off, dressed, and race to our next class—I just hated it. I'd try to get out of it all the time. One time I played sick. "I don't feel good," I told the teacher.

She said, "Fine. Go sit by the bleachers."

I thought this was pretty good and thought I found my way out of swimming class for the rest of the year. The next week I said to the teacher: "I don't feel good again." And I got to stay dry again. And so I tried it again and again. Then the teacher got mad. One week I went up to her and said: "I don't feel good." And this time, she wasn't having any of it. "How many times don't you feel good?" she said. "Go take off your clothes and get into the pool!"

We didn't have a lot of fish during the Depression because it was expensive, but we were able to get our hands on smelts from time to time. I like cooking with smelts because they are delicious and cheap. When you fry them up this way, they taste like French fries. Some people say they're like bait fish, and they kind of are. They're also a lot like sardines—and you can also use this recipe to prepare sardines if you like those, too. What I like about them is

that you're supposed to eat every last bit of them. Too bad, I guess, for any stray cats you might have living with you.

You will need

1 pound frozen smelts

1 cup all-purpose flour

1 tablespoon salt

1 teaspoon pepper

½ cup vegetable oil

1. Put the smelts into a bowl of cold water to thaw. Spread out the flour on a dish and season with the salt and pepper.

2. In a large frying pan, heat the oil over medium to medium-high heat. While the oil heats, dredge the fish in the flour, shaking off any excess.

3. Fry up the smelts in batches, till they're nice and golden brown, about 4 minutes per side.

4. Drain on paper towels to absorb excess oil. Season with additional salt, if desired, and serve hot.

Roast Beef

· Serves 4 to 6 ·

I LIKE THE OLD WAYS, and I always did. Even back then, I didn't like change too much. I like scrubbing the floor clean on my hands and knees with a hard-bristled brush. It doesn't get clean any other way. Sure, there were some things that made life easier, but some things I never really trusted. Like cars. My uncle had a car because he owned a store. He was rich. We didn't have a car or even a horse. In fact I never learned to drive and neither did my parents.

I remember when the cars started coming to our neighborhood, like the Model T. It was the only car you would see. Back then there were more horses on the road than cars. It was a big event if someone got a car. The whole neighborhood would be gathered around the new Ford. Then we would pile in, seven at a time, and get a ride around the block.

The cars used to have a crank in the front and the driver would have to get out and crank it up before we got going. It would go *brah-brum, brum, brum* and then start up. Sometimes it wouldn't start right away and the driver would be at it for ten, twenty minutes.

The roads were bumpy because they weren't paved. If they weren't dirt roads they were either brick or cobblestone. They were also very wet from all of the horse droppings. You had to be real careful when getting out of a car back then.

Today everything seems to happen so fast and it's hard to sit back and appreciate things. But a slow-cooked meal gives you something to celebrate. It's better for you than something quick, and because it takes so long to make, you enjoy it more. When we used to come in the house when something special was cooking, the smell was so good. I still remember the smell of my mother's roast beef, which we only had for the most special occasions. It was simple and delicious. Here's how she did it.

You will need

One 3- to 4-pound round or sirloin tip beef roast
¼ cup olive oil
Salt and pepper

1. Preheat the oven to 500°F.

2. Rinse the roast quickly under cold running water and pat dry. Rub the roast all over with olive oil and sprinkle it with salt and pepper. Place the roast in a roasting pan, fat side up, and then in the preheated oven.

3. Roast at 500°F for 20 minutes to sear the meat. Then lower the oven temperature to 300°F.

4. Continue roasting for approximately 20 minutes per pound. If you like it well done, then roast it for 23 to 25 minutes per pound.

5. Remove the roast from the oven and let it rest for 10 to 15 minutes before carving. Serve and enjoy.

Roast Beef Stew

· **Serves 4 to 6** ·

S AM AND I each only had two pairs of shoes: one to wear all the time, one to wear on Sundays. The ones we wore every day were nothing special, but I loved the ones I had for Sundays. They were patent leather and were always shiny—they had to be. That was one of our jobs Saturday mornings. We had to polish all our shoes (weekday shoes, too), along with our parents' shoes, and line them up for my mother to inspect. My mother would inspect them, and if we passed, we'd get our allowance, which was about a nickel when we were kids and a dime when we got older.

Shining the shoes wasn't the only thing we had to do. Because of my mother's arthritis, Sam and I had to scrub down the house every Saturday morning, which meant no sleeping in. I hated that. I always hated getting up, especially on Saturdays.

"Mom, can't I sleep in?" I'd whine. "It's Saturday."

And she'd shout up the stairs: "NO!"

So we'd get up and we'd scrub down the house and then we'd shine the shoes and line them up. And while we cleaned, Ma would be cooking up something slow and special. Everything had to be clean by noon on Saturday. And then, only after my mother was satisfied, we could eat.

Mom would sometimes make this from the part of the roast she hid away, but you can make it with regular stew beef if you want. It's delicious served with Ma's fresh bread.

You will need

2 tablespoons olive oil
2 pounds beef stew meat, cut into 1-inch cubes
1 onion, sliced
2 cloves garlic, minced
6 carrots, peeled and roughly chopped
3 celery stalks, roughly chopped
One 28-ounce can chopped tomatoes
4 medium potatoes, peeled and cubed
1 teaspoon salt
½ teaspoon pepper

1. In a large covered pot set on high heat, heat the olive oil, add the meat, and brown the meat on all sides. Remove with a slotted spoon and set aside.

2. Lower the heat to medium and add the onion. Sauté, stirring occasionally, for about 8 to 10 minutes. Add the garlic for the last 2 minutes. Add the carrots and celery, and continue frying for 10 more minutes, stirring occasionally.

3. Add the tomatoes and beef and bring to a boil. Lower heat to a simmer and add the potatoes and salt and pepper.

4. Simmer on low heat for 2½ to 3 hours. Remove from the heat and serve piping hot with fresh bread.

CHAPTER SIX

Sweet Rewards

W E DIDN'T HAVE MUCH to look forward to at the end of the day. We had lots of work at school and at work, and then there was all we had to do around the house. But every now and then we'd treat ourselves. When I was a kid, it was dessert I looked forward to, which we only had on Sundays really.

When I was older, it was dancing I looked forward to. A group of us would head to the Aragon and the Trianon, which were the big dance halls in Chicago. They'd have singers and an orchestra and once there was a little skinny guy named Frank Sinatra up there on the stage. This was in the late 1930s, and we were finally coming out of the dark days, but we'd still have to save for weeks to have enough money for one night of dancing.

I used to go with one of my girlfriends, who was dating a boy from the neighborhood her parents didn't approve of. So I'd go with her and she would dance with her boyfriend and I would stand there and wait for dances with other guys. The dance would go until midnight and then we would go back home on the streetcar.

One night I went with a whole bunch of friends from the neighborhood. There must have been eight of us. My cousin Mimi and all of her cousins and brothers. We were the only girls. One of the guys had a car, so we all piled into it after the dance hall closed. It was so foggy out that we couldn't see the road at all. Joe was driving and he opened up his door to see where the lines of the road were. He was looking with the door open and a cop stopped us.

"Where you going?" He was real upset.

"We were at the Aragon and now we are going home," said Joe.

"How come you opened up the door!?"

"Well, I couldn't see with the fog, so I opened the door just to see where the road lines were."

The cop looks at Mimi and me piled in with all those guys. "What are you doing with all these men?"

Mimi was nervous and started pointing at all the guys, "That's my brother, that's my cousin, that's my cousin, that's my uncle!"

The cop narrowed his eyes at her and said, "Yeah, and I'm your father."

I said, "No, she's telling the truth."

He didn't believe us, but he let us go anyways.

There aren't any dance halls anymore that you can do this at. It's too bad. I used to love to dance. I'd like to dance still.

Anyhow, the point is that times were tough, but if we saved up for our rewards, when we got to have them—a night out dancing or a delicious dessert—you can just imagine how sweet they tasted to us.

Cherry Jam on Bread

Serves 4; makes 3 pints jam

I'M NOT A MORNING PERSON now and I never have been. I still remember what mornings were like in our house. We'd wake up to a little warm light outside our door. It was our second oil lamp. We had only two of them—one for the upstairs and one for the downstairs. When we opened our eyes and saw that lamp on, we knew that if we didn't get up now Ma was going to start hollering.

There was no light in the bathroom, so we would leave the door open so we could see. We had running water, but we didn't take a bath or shower in the mornings in those days, so it didn't really matter that the door was open. We just washed our faces, neck, ears, under our arms. My mother was crazy about cleanliness, though, and always made sure I washed up good. She'd stand over me and if I wasn't scrubbing right she'd shout: "Not like that, like this!" And then she would take over the scrubbing and scrub real hard.

Ma was always hovering. I wanted to fall back to sleep, but she was always all over me. My brother would get up real easy, but I was the lazy one and that's why I got so much attention. Then we would brush our teeth. "Don't use so much toothpaste!" she'd holler. She always made sure we went real easy on the soap and toothpaste, it had to last a real long time.

It didn't matter all the other things she had to do in the morning. For her, the most important thing was that her kids were clean. In fact, that's what the nuns at school said to us, too. They always made an example of my brother and me. Lots of kids came to school with ratty-looking clothes and holes in their stockings. Not us. "You can be poor, but you can be clean," they would say, pointing to us.

Our clothing was about as basic as our food, back when I was growing up. The girls would wear one-piece dresses and the boys would wear a button-up shirt, pants with a belt, and hard leather shoes. If it was cold we would wear a sweater over the dress or shirt, and galoshes if it rained or snowed. But nothing ever too fancy. Even on Sundays.

Then we'd head down to breakfast, which was always a slice of Ma's bread with coffee. Some mornings we had butter on the bread. And some mornings, I guess if we were good, Ma would open one of her jars of homemade cherry jam. That was really special.

You will need

> 3 pounds sour cherries, pitted
> Zest of 2 lemons
> Juice of 2 lemons
> 2½ cups sugar
> 4 slices bread

1. Cook the cherries in a large (16- to 20-quart) pot over medium to high heat until they are soft, about 20 minutes, stirring occasionally.

2. Add the lemon zest and juice and stir to combine. Add the sugar and stir it into the cherries until dissolved. Continue stirring the cherries, scraping the bottom of the pot as you stir, and cook over moderate to high heat for an additional 20 to 30 minutes.

3. When the cherry and sugar mixture thickens into a jam thick enough to coat the spoon or spatula, remove the pot from the heat.

4. Spoon the jam into sterilized jars and let them cool to room temperature. Once they have cooled, cover and refrigerate.

5. Once the jam has been refrigerated at least overnight, spread it on your bread and enjoy!

Italian Ice

W E DIDN'T HAVE MONEY like kids do today. We didn't get everything we wanted, so when we had a treat, it was really special.

Each Saturday we cleaned the house, so Sunday was our one day of rest. Our parents wanted us out of their hair, so they gave us each a nickel and we ran out of the house to spend it. And we celebrated with it the way kids do: with ice cream. There was an ice cream parlor on Lake Street and they knew all of us kids from the neighborhood there.

It was Italian-owned, so it was probably gelato. But every Sunday we'd show up there with our nickels and get our ice cream. Vanilla was my favorite. I think they only opened that place on Sundays. I can't imagine when they would have done any other business. But it was packed on Sundays. That was for sure.

We'd also have ice cream and also Italian ices at the festival. My second cousin Rose Cappello would roll out a big barrel of Italian ice outside the front of her grocery store. The ice was frozen solid, and Rose and her two sons, Sam and Tony, would spend all day scraping it out. It was a popular spot during the festivals, and I would hang around her, asking for a free cup. Even though we were related, when I asked her for a cup she would reply with the price. She was a real businesswoman. She had only one flavor, vanilla, and it was my favorite. When we got down to the bottom of the barrel it got nice and soft. I'll never forget how good it tasted on a hot summer evening.

You will need

> 2 cups water
> ½ cup sugar
> 2 teaspoons pure clear vanilla extract
> 4 fresh mint leaves

1. Pour the water and sugar into a small pot and bring to a boil. Let the sugar dissolve evenly for about 5 minutes, then remove from the heat.

2. Place the pot in the freezer and leave it there for 4 to 5 hours. Give the mixture a few turns with a metal spoon every half hour or so, keeping the mixture from freezing completely.

3. Remove the pot from the freezer. Scrape the ice with a metal spoon into a medium bowl. The ice should shave off nicely. At the bottom of the pot the ice will be a little more frozen, so mash it up with your spoon.

4. When all the ice is in the bowl, add the vanilla and mix well. Spoon the ice into four small glass dishes and return them to the freezer for 15 minutes. Remove from the freezer, top each glass with a leaf of fresh mint, and serve immediately.

Fresh Milk Custard Pudding

• Serves 2 •

W E DIDN'T GET OUR MILK in the grocery store. It was my job when we needed milk to go get it from the woman who had the cow down the street. I loved the cream on the top of the milk, and sometimes I'd drink it on my way back home. I'd replace the missing part with water from the basement, but I had to be careful. If I ever got caught I'd get such a lickin'. Like we did whenever we spilled sugar. It was expensive and every bit mattered. But that cream was so good, it was always worth the risk. If there was ever any extra cream, Mom would sometimes whip up a warm custard for me and my brother. Not having that made me want to kick myself sometimes for drinking all the cream. It was a nice treat.

You will need

> 2 large eggs
> ¼ cup sugar
> 1 cup heavy cream
> Ground cinnamon

1. Preheat the oven to 350°F. Fill a cake pan halfway with warm water and set aside.

2. In a medium bowl, beat the eggs with the sugar. Slowly add the cream and whisk with a fork.

3. Pour the custard into two oven-safe mugs, or ramekins if you have them, and place the mugs in the cake pan. Place the pan in the preheated oven and bake the custard, stirring now and then for the first 20 minutes. Bake an additional 40 minutes, or until the custard sets.

4. Let the custards cool for 45 minutes to 1 hour. Dust the tops with cinnamon, and serve.

Take It from Me

Always use the stairs. People tell me that I shouldn't be going up and down my stairs at my age, but I need them— they keep me limber. So what if we wear out our shoes if we keep ourselves fit?

Baked Sugar Apples

• Serves 4 •

I N MY NEIGHBORHOOD, you knew it was time to pick apples when the fruit truck honked its horn. We didn't get our apples from the tree, but you had to work just as hard to get the best ones. The fruit truck would park and put out wooden steps so you could walk right inside of it. There would be rows of fruit on either side, in crates or out on display.

The women in the neighborhood would wait for the truck to park and put down the steps and then, like mad-women, they would shove their way into the back of the

truck. The fruit man would laugh and say, "Ladies, ladies, two at a time, you're going to break the truck." The whole truck would be rocking back and forth, but that's the only way you would get first picking.

One of my favorite ways Ma used some of the cheaper, not the best, apples was to make this dessert. Use the caramel formed from the sugar and juice of the apples to drizzle over the apple (or vanilla ice cream, if you are lucky), before serving.

You will need

4 large baking apples

2 tablespoons butter

8 tablespoons sugar

2 heaping teaspoons ground cinnamon

1. Preheat the oven to 350°F and cover a baking sheet with a piece of aluminum foil. Core the apples straight through to the bottom.

2. Cut 1 tablespoon of the butter into quarters and place the quarters on the baking sheet. Top with the apples, placing 2 tablespoons of sugar and ½ teaspoon of cinnamon in each apple. Top each apple with another ¼ tablespoon of butter.

3. Bake the apples in the center of the oven for 45 minutes, or until tender.

Sugar Cookies

OR BREAKFAST, WE usually only had bread with butter and coffee. We used to dip our bread in the coffee and eat it. We always had evaporated milk. But sometimes on Sundays we'd have these special sugar cookies, which Ma baked that morning, with our coffee. That was a real treat.

Sunday really was the sweetest day of the week. We'd always have some kind of dessert on Sundays. Sometimes my aunt would bring us a box of sugar wafer cookies. My brother and I would count them out one by one, and divide them evenly. If there was an extra, we'd cut it in half. We'd have them with a little coffee. Ma didn't want us to have a lot of coffee, so she'd give us a drop of coffee and mostly milk. But we had our cookies, day and night, so we were happy.

You will need

> ¾ cup sugar
> ¾ cup (1½ sticks) butter
> 3 large eggs
> 3 cups all-purpose flour
> Pinch of salt

1. Preheat the oven to 350°F.

2. Cream the sugar and butter together in a medium bowl. In a separate bowl, whisk the eggs, then mix them in with the creamed butter.

3. Add about 1½ cups flour and mix it into the batter until the flour disappears. Work the batter into a dough, adding the rest of the flour as necessary, about 1½ cups more.

4. On a clean work surface or board spread out an even coating of flour. Take a handful of dough and roll it out in the flour, shaping it into a roll.

5. Cut each of the rolls into 3-inch sections, giving the smaller sections each a couple of small cuts in the middle, and then curling the sections into half-moons.

6. Place the cookies on an ungreased cookie sheet (I don't use grease on the pans because the dough's got enough grease) and bake at 350°F until golden brown, 13 to 15 minutes.

7. Remove the cookies from the oven and cool at least 30 minutes before eating.

Take It from Me

When you're rolling out your dough, be generous with the flour on the work surface so the dough doesn't stick.

Mom's Simple Cake

· Serves 6 to 8 ·

NO ONE EVER celebrated your birthday back in the old days. Birthdays were nothing, not like they are today. We didn't have birthday cakes. The day came and went. Someone said, "Happy Birthday." That was it. We went without having a lot of things, but we were happy—we didn't know what we were missing because we didn't think we should have it. For my mother's birthday, we had to do something. We at least had to give her a present, something like a blouse or a scarf. But we never got anything.

Forget about birthdays, though. Cakes, for any occasion, didn't really exist in our house during the Depression. Ma would only make a simple cake if she had the ingredients left over from another recipe. It was a nice treat, but it didn't come with candles and a song. The only thing special for us kids on our birthdays was that we got to request our favorite meal.

We were too young to bake my mother a cake, and we knew if we messed it up and wasted the food Mom wouldn't be very cheery on her birthday. Instead we would make her birthday cards. We would make several, since most other families had so many kids we wanted her to feel just as special with just the two of us. Even the colors were simpler back then. Instead of having sixty-four crayons, we made do with four. But despite the limitations, Ma usually wore a nice smile the whole day.

Ma had a recipe for a simple cake, and it holds up pretty well even today. It makes a small, thin cake, but it's still delicious.

You will need

1 stick (½ cup) butter

½ cup sugar

1 large egg

1 teaspoon pure vanilla extract

¾ cup all-purpose flour

¾ teaspoon baking powder

¼ cup milk

½ teaspoon powdered sugar

¼ teaspoon ground cinnamon

1. Preheat the oven to 350°F. Grease and flour a 9 × 5 × 2¾-inch bread pan, completely coating the bottom and all the way up the sides of the pan so the dough doesn't stick when it rises.

2. In a bowl, cream together the butter and sugar. Beat in the egg and stir in the vanilla.

3. In a separate bowl, combine the flour and baking powder and slowly add them to the sugar mixture. Mix well. Now add the milk and mix until the batter is nice and smooth.

4. Pour into the prepared cake pan and bake at 350°F for 20 minutes. The cake is done when the top is golden.

5. Remove the cake from the oven and let it cool on a rack.

6. When cool, gently remove the cake from the pan and transfer it to a serving plate. Sprinkle the top of the cake with the powdered sugar and cinnamon and serve.

Aunt Lucy's Sponge Cake

· Serves 12 ·

F AMILY WAS VERY IMPORTANT TO US. It was one of the only things we had, and what kept us grounded. Some of the best times we had were the times when we were all together. It didn't matter what we were doing. During the holidays or just on a weekend afternoon, the whole point was just being together. There doesn't seem to be as much of that going on today. People are so busy. But family is everything.

Most of the people I knew growing up are gone now. It's really just me and Sam. But there are generations past

us that still get together all the time. No matter what, my family still tries and makes time to be together, even these days. It's a big part of what's been keeping me going all these years!

Early on, we didn't have a radio, but we went to our aunts' and uncles' houses, and all gathered around to listen to our family's storytellers. Back then, you didn't buy whole books, you bought chapters. My aunt Lucia, whom we usually just called Aunt Lucy, always bought a few chapters a month of her favorite stories, which were romances. She was a great reader and we would look forward to her reading aloud from the serials she would get. Entertainment wasn't as easily available then as it is now, but it didn't matter. We were happy to have it any way we could get it. Those were good times.

It was always cold in her house, so to go there, we'd dress up real warm. When we got there she'd always have something warm for us to drink. That made our day.

On a Sunday afternoon, after a simple meal, Aunt Lucy would sometimes have a special treat for us: her famous sponge cake. It wasn't fancy and we didn't care. It was light and sweet and a perfect treat and we all ate as much of it as we could. Sometimes, on a good week, she'd top it with chocolate or preserves, if these were available, or sometimes just a light dusting of powdered sugar—and you may decide to finish off your cake with something like this. But sometimes her cake had no topping at all and it never mattered. It was delicious just as it was.

Take It from Me

Clarified butter sounds a lot more complicated than it is. It's really easy to make. Just melt some butter and see how it divides up with the clear yellow at the bottom and the white skin on the top? Skim off the white part with a spoon and there you have it: The yellow part is now clarified.

You will need

6 whole large eggs
6 egg yolks
1 cup sugar
1 cup all-purpose flour, sifted
½ cup clarified butter, cooled
1 teaspoon pure vanilla extract

1. Preheat the oven to 350°F. Grease and lightly flour 2 9-inch round cake pans.

2. Combine the eggs, egg yolks, and sugar together in a small bowl.

3. Fill a saucepan a little less than half-full with water and place it over medium heat on the stove. The saucepan should be small enough that the bowl with the egg and sugar mixture can rest inside it and not submerge.

4. Reduce the heat to low and place the bowl with the egg and sugar mixture in the saucepan. Whisk the egg and sugar mixture continuously as it warms, about 2 minutes.

5. Remove the mixture from the heat and beat with an electric mixer at high speed for about 15 minutes, until it's fluffy like whipped cream.

6. Sprinkle the flour onto the mixture, followed by the clarified butter and then the vanilla. Delicately, with a wooden spoon or rubber spatula, fold all the ingredients together.

7. Pour the batter into your cake pans and bake at 350°F for 25 to 30 minutes. The cake is done when it is lightly brown and separates from the sides of the pan.

8. Remove the cake from the pans and cool. Frost as desired or sprinkle with powdered sugar.

Sugared Nuts

• Makes 1 cup •

Nuts were expensive, so this was a special treat we could have if there was ever any extra money at the end of the week—though you can bet there wasn't. I hate to admit it, but this was partly my fault.

We only had one pair of shoes to wear the whole week, but I was really hard on shoes and I'd break them all the time. Part of the reason is that I walked everywhere and I just wore them down. Part of the reason was that I played like a maniac and the shoes weren't built for someone with all the energy I had. So they fell apart all the time. Lucky for me, there was a man who lived down the street who fixed shoes. Whenever I'd break mine, I'd run to him.

He was always so patient with me. "What'd you do this time?" he'd ask.

And I'd show him how my strap broke or my sole was hanging off. "You gotta help me, please," I'd say. "If my mother sees this, she'll give me a lickin'."

Then he'd feel sorry for me and he'd fix my shoe and say, "Never again. You're on your own the next time."

And I'd nod my head. And we both knew I'd be back again in a couple of days.

You will need

1/2 cup shelled almonds
1/2 cup shelled pecans
1/4 cup sugar
1 tablespoon butter
1/4 teaspoon salt

1. Put the ingredients into a small saucepan (not non-stick). Place a sheet of wax paper on your countertop.

2. Place the pan over medium heat, and stir everything together. Don't stop stirring the nuts or the caramel will become uneven. After about 12 minutes of constant stirring, the caramel will turn a golden brown.

3. Remove the nuts from the heat and pour out onto the wax paper. Let cool for at least 15 minutes.

Holiday Biscotti

W E ENJOYED THE HOLIDAYS growing up but not be-cause we liked all the toys. Which is good because we didn't get a lot of toys. In fact, most years we didn't get any at all. We'd still get presents, though. We'd open them before Mass. Then my whole extended family would go to Mass together and come back to one of our homes and eat sausage sandwiches. That's about all.

My mother would buy a present for each of the kids, maybe a hat or a pair of gloves. Each of my cousins got some-thing a little special. But that wasn't the case for us from my aunt's family. Every year they used to buy us all the same

thing, a box of chocolates that cost a quarter. As soon as I saw the shape of that box I'd say, "That's for me." And sure enough, it was either for my brother or me. We used to get about six or seven boxes of chocolates every year. I was so disappointed sometimes. I really wished that for once they would put some thought into what they gave. So sometimes when we'd go home I'd cry.

During the Depression, there were no gifts or celebrations at all for the holidays. For us, it was all about the family being together. So I guess I really missed those chocolates then. But we still had plenty of sweets. Even during the Depression, Ma would find a way to make something special, like her biscotti. Most of the time she made them plain, but if it was a good year, we might even be able to look forward to chocolate on our biscotti. Here's how she made them.

You will need

2 cups all-purpose flour
¾ cup sugar
¼ teaspoon salt
¼ teaspoon ground cinnamon
1 tablespoon vegetable oil
3 large eggs
¼ cup shelled almonds, chopped

Take It from Me

Whole almonds are nice, but chopping them up makes them go much further.

1. Preheat the oven to 375°F.

2. Combine the flour, sugar, salt, cinnamon, and oil in a bowl, and mix in the eggs, one at a time. Once the ingredients are incorporated into a dough, add the chopped almonds.

3. Divide the dough into two rectangular pieces. Lightly flour the surface you will be working on and roll the dough pieces with your hands into logs about 12 inches long and 1 inch in diameter. Place the logs on a cookie sheet and bake in the preheated oven for 15 to 20 minutes, until the edges are lightly golden brown.

4. Remove the two logs from the cookie sheet and cool on a cutting board for 10 to 15 minutes. When cool, slice them into diagonal pieces, about the thickness of two fingers.

5. Reduce the oven heat to 300°F and raise the oven rack to the top slot. Place the individual biscotti back on the cookie sheet, cut side down.

6. Bake until the tops become a golden color, 8 to 10 minutes, then turn them over and bake an additional 8 to 10 minutes, until the biscotti are golden brown.

Chocolate Glaze

This glaze makes the cookies extra special.

You will need

½ cup condensed milk (or fresh if you prefer)

½ teaspoon sugar

2 tablespoons cocoa powder

1 tablespoon butter, melted

1. Combine the milk, sugar, and cocoa powder in a small saucepan over low heat.

2. Pour the melted butter into the cocoa mixture and wait for it to slowly bubble. Stir slowly and continuously until the milk reduces, about 7 minutes.

3. Remove the glaze from the heat and dip the cooled biscotti into the chocolate. Allow the glaze to cool and harden before serving.

Holiday Fig Cookies (Cucidati)

• Yields 6 to 8 dozen •

A FTER THE DEPRESSION WAS OVER, these cookies were a very special treat we used to make about once a year, and still do. We never once made them during the Depression. You couldn't have made them then if you wanted to because there are too many ingredients and they're all expensive. So you have to wait until after the hard times are over to make cookies this good. But at least that gives you something to look forward to.

This dessert is delicious but takes a lot of time and a lot of work. What's nice about it is that one person can't do it alone. You need at least a couple of willing family members to work on it with you, which gives you some nice family time.

I think my family recipe is still the best one. Once I was in a bakery where they were selling these cookies. I talked to the man who owned the store to find out how he made his. I looked at them a minute and said: "Mine are better."

"I don't believe you," he said.

So I told him next time I made them, I'd bring one in for him and he could see for himself, and I did. He took a bite and said, "I have to admit they are better."

The last time I made these cookies, I was carrying them on a tray down the stairs. I was walking down the stairs backwards and I fell. There were these ladies there and one of them asked: "Did you drop a cookie?" Did I drop any?

Then the other one said, "You know, there's a spider web down there."

"Spider web? I just fell down the stairs here!" Everyone really cared a lot about those cookies.

Take It from Me

Use fresh nuts, right from the shell, for this recipe. It takes some time to shell all those nuts, but everyone likes them better so it's worth the extra work—and extra time spent with your kids or grandkids.

For the Filling

You will need

¾ cup shelled hazelnuts

½ cup shelled almonds

½ cup shelled walnuts

½ cup shelled pecans

2 cups water

½ cup sugar

½ pound diced candied fruit

¼ pound dark raisins

¼ pound light raisins

¼ pound pitted dates

1 orange with rind, sliced

1 tangerine rind, dried out at room temperature

2 pounds figs or two 14-ounce packages dried figs

½ cup whiskey

1. Preheat the oven to 350°F. Pour the nuts out in a single layer on a baking sheet and toast in the oven until golden, 10 to 15 minutes.

2. Bring the water to a boil and when boiling, add the sugar. Set aside.

3. In a large bowl, using your hands, mix together the nuts, candied fruit, dark raisins, light raisins, dates, figs, orange slices, and dried tangerine rind.

4. In batches, grind the mixture to a fine paste in a food processor. Return the paste to the bowl and stir in the sugar-water and whiskey. Cover and refrigerate overnight.

5. Before you begin the dough in the next part, take this mixture out of the refrigerator so that it has settled to room temperature when you're ready to use it to fill the cookies.

Take It from Me

Have your grandchildren take you out to dinner after you make the filling for the cookies, and share some stories from your childhood with them. They want to hear about these more than they let on sometimes.

For the Dough

You will need

10 cups all-purpose flour

1 cup lard, broken up

1½ cups sugar

1 cup cold milk

2 heaping tablespoons baking powder

1 tablespoon pure vanilla extract

12 large eggs, beaten

1. Preheat the oven to 350°F.

2. In a large bowl, combine all the ingredients, one by one, and, with your hands, mix until you get a nice, pliable dough. Cover with a clean dish towel, set aside, and let stand, at room temperature, for about 1 hour.

3. Start working the dough again. If it's too soft, add a bit more flour to make it more sturdy.

4. Dust a clean work surface with flour and take out a big piece of dough. Roll it out thin with a rolling pin. Keep wetting your hands so that they don't stick to the dough.

For the Cookies

1. Start spooning out the filling in a straight line on the dough. Fold the dough over the filling to create a nice roll. Cut the dough and press in the sides. Repeat to make more rolls.

2. Take the filled rolls and cut them into three or four 3-inch rolls. Make a couple of small cuts in each of these smaller rolls, on the diagonal. Place on an ungreased cookie sheet (the dough will be greasy enough that the cookies won't stick).

3. Bake the cucidati first on the lower rack of the oven for 10 to 13 minutes. Then, when they're nice and rosy, move them to a higher rack, and finish baking for an additional 5 minutes, or until golden.

4. Lay out the cookies for a few hours to cool before icing. (If I'm making as many as these, I usually lay them out over a sheet on the bed.)

Take It from Me

These cookies are lots of work and I don't know if it's worth it. But when I see how much my family enjoys them, I realize it's worth the extra effort once a year.

For the Icing

You will need

2 tablespoons milk
2 cups sifted powdered sugar
1 teaspoon pure clear vanilla extract
Colored sprinkles

1. Mix the milk with the powdered sugar and blend. Add the vanilla. Be sure to use pure clear vanilla extract or it will ruin the color of the icing.

2. Spread the icing over the cooled cookies. Let your grandchildren add the sprinkles to the cookies.

3. Let set for 15 minutes and enjoy.

Take It from Me

It's amazing—all that work and you take one bite and the thing is gone. These cookies are sweet and really good for you when you're constipated. They really work good. It's all the figs, I guess.

Thanks for spending some time with me in my kitchen and listening to all my stories. I hope you'll enjoy the recipes I've shared here as much as my family and I have for generations. I also hope that learning how we survived the Great Depression will help you survive your own tough times. What will get you through is just what got us through—family and friends, and finding joy wherever you can. Remember, there's nothing like sharing a nice plate of pasta with the people you love to brighten even the darkest days.

Good luck

Clara

Select List of Illustrations

Index

L

M

N

O

P

11/09